John Howard Brown

Bryan, Sewall and Honest Money Will Bring Prosperity

John Howard Brown

Bryan, Sewall and Honest Money Will Bring Prosperity

ISBN/EAN: 9783744731492

Printed in Europe, USA, Canada, Australia, Japan

Cover: Foto ©Lupo / pixelio.de

More available books at **www.hansebooks.com**

WILLIAM JENNINGS BRYAN.

Bryan, Sewall and Honest Money

WILL BRING

PROSPERITY.

"THE CRIME OF SEVENTY-THREE."
WHO WAS THE CRIMINAL?

BIMETALLISM THE ONLY REMEDY FOR HARD TIMES. IT WAS A *SUCCESS* FROM **1792** TO **1873**, AND THEREFORE IS NOT AN *EXPERIMENT*.

" The free and unlimited coinage of silver at the ratio of 16 to 1, without waiting for the aid or consent of any nation on earth.

" A dollar that increases in value is just as dishonest as a dollar that decreases in value." —W. J. BRYAN.

" I concur with you that the unit must stand on both metals." —*Letter of JEFFERSON to HAMILTON, Feb., 1792.*

JOHN HOWARD BROWN,

Editor " National Portrait Gallery," " National Cyclopædia of American Biography," Author " American Naval Heroes," etc.

PORTRAITS OF THE LEADERS IN THE MOVEMENT FOR THE RESTORATION OF SILVER TO ITS OLD PLACE AS A STANDARD OF VALUE. PLATFORM, SPEECHES, BIOGRAPHIES, ARGUMENTS, STATISTICS.

New York:
DERBY AND MILLER COMPANY.
1896.

"We live in a land where every year presents a battlefield and every day a call to duty."—W. J. Bryan.

"We know that that which is right will finally triumph, because there is nothing omnipotent but truth."—W. J. Bryan.

PRESS OF
JENKINS & McCOWAN,
NEW YORK.

FREE SILVER AND NATIONAL PROSPERITY.

The address delivered by Mr. William P. St. John on accepting the permanent chairmanship of the National Bimetallic party at St. Louis, July 22, 1896.

By WILLIAM P. ST. JOHN, M. A.

It is among the first principles in finance that the value of each dollar expressed in prices, depends upon the total number of dollars in circulation. The plane of prices is high when the number of dollars in circulation is great in proportion to the number of things to be exchanged by means of dollars, and low when the dollars are proportionately few. The plane of prices at present and for some time past is and has been ruinously low.

The increase of our population at about two millions a year, scattered over our immense territory, calls for increasing exchanges and thereby demands an increasing number of dollars in circulation. The increase in the number of dollars when dollars are confined to gold is not sufficiently rapid to meet the growth of our exchanges. The consequence is a growing value of dollars or a diminishing value of everything else expressed in dollars ; which is to say a tendency toward constantly declining prices.

The fountain-head of our prosperity has run dry. Our farmers all over the country have endured the depression in prices, until they get about $8 or $9 per acre for an expenditure of $10 per acre and the like. Their credit is exhausted at the country stores. The country store ceases to order from the city merchant, the city merchant reduces his demand upon the manufacturer. Manufactures are curtailed.

The consequence is that employees and all elements of labor

5

are being discharged, and wages are lowered to those who continue in employment. The sufferings of the farmers, who constitute nearly one-half of our population, are thus enforced upon the city merchant, the manufacturer, and all forms of labor. These combined elements constitute the overwhelming majority of voters. Their intelligent conclusion will be felt when expressed at the polls.

The banker also is without prosperity unless prosperity is general throughout the United States. He must learn to distinguish between cheap money and money commanding a low rate of interest. The dollar worth two bushels of wheat is a dear dollar, and yet it commands interest in Wall Street at present of but 2 per cent. per annum on call. If the dollar can be cheapened by increasing the number of dollars, so that each dollar will buy less wheat, the increasing price of wheat will increase the demand for dollars to invest in its production.

Then the borrower of dollars to invest in the production of wheat, being reasonably sure of a profit from that employment of the money, can afford to pay interest for its use as a part of his profit. In other words, interest is a share of the profit on the employment of money. So that abundant money, money readily obtainable, which is to say really cheap money, is the money which commands a high rate of interest as a share of the profit of the borrower in using it.

As we appeal to the country, in the justice of our cause, one or two points of common inquiry must be satisfied as follows:

The experience of Mexico is held up for our alarm. We answer, first, that Mexico is conspicuously prosperous at home. Her increase in manufactures, railway earnings, and the like in recent years is phenomenal. Second, Mexico is no criterion for the United States, for the reason that she has a foreign trade indebtedness of about $20,000,000 annually in excess of the value of her exports of cotton, sugar, coffee, hides, and the like, which must be paid for in the surplus product of her mines. Her silver, therefore, goes abroad as merchandise and at a valuation fixed by the outside world.

The United States, on the other hand, is a nation of seventy millions of people, scattered over a territory seventeen times the area of France. A single one of our railway systems, the Erie, exceeds the aggregate railway mileage of all Mexico. We offer an employment for money to an aggregate greater than the world's spare silver will furnish us. Hence our silver money, at home and abroad, will be valued as the money of the United States.

The opposition threatens us with a flood of Europe's silver upon our reopened mints. We answer, Europe has no silver but her silver money. Her silver money values silver at from 3 to 7 cents on the dollar higher than ours. Hence the European merchant or banker must sacrifice from 3 to 7 per cent. of his full legal-tender money in order to recoin it at our mints. Europe's silverware, like America's silverware, carries in it the additional value of labor and the manufacturer's profit.

They threaten us with a flood of silver from the far East. We answer that the course of silver is invariably eastward, and never toward the west. British India is a perpetual sink of silver, absorbing it, never to return, by from $30,000,000 to $60,000,000 worth every year. And India's absorption of silver will be enlarged by the steadiness of price for silver fixed by our reopened mints.

They threaten us with a " sudden retirement of $600,000,000 gold, with the accompanying panic, causing contraction and commercial disaster unparalleled." We answer that our total stock of gold, other than about $10,000,000 or $15,000,000 circulating on the Pacific coast, is already in retirement. Practically all our gold is in the United States Treasury, or held by banks.

The gold in the treasury will remain there if the Secretary avails himself of his option to redeem United States notes in silver.

The gold in the banks constitutes the quiet and undisturbed portion of their reserves against their liabilities. It will continue to do money duty as such reserves after free coinage for silver is enacted. Hence a premium on it will not contract the currency. The utmost possible contraction of the currency will be the few millions circulating on the Pacific coast, and this will be retired but slowly.

A similar threat of a flight of gold was made for the Bland Act of 1878. President Hayes was urged to veto it, but Congress passed it over the veto. Instead of a flight of gold, as had been predicted, we gained by importation $4,000,000 the first year, $70,000,000 the next, and $90,000,000 the third year. During the twelve years that the act was on the statute book we gained $221,-000,000 of foreign gold.

Instead of the destruction of our credit abroad, as had been predicted, the United States 4 per cent. loan, which stood at 101 on the day of the enactment, sold at 120 per cent. within three years, and at 130 per cent. subsequently. Instead of defeating the resumption of specie payments on January 1st of the following year, the 24,000,000 silver dollars which were coined in 1878, and circulated by means of the silver certificates, reduced the demand upon the government for gold. Hence the threat of disaster now is without historic foundation.

This, then, is what will follow the reopening of our mints to silver : The gold already in the treasury will remain there, if common sense dictates the treasury management; that is, if the Treasurer exercises the option to redeem United States notes in silver. A premium on gold will not occasion a contraction of the currency, bank hoards of gold continuing to serve as a portion of bank reserves against bank liabilities. A premium on gold will tend to increase our exports by causing a higher rate of foreign exchange; that is to say, by yielding a larger net return in dollars on the sale of bills of exchange drawn against goods exported. A premium will tend to diminish our imports by increasing the cost of bills of exchange with which to pay for our goods imported.

The tendency of increasing our exports and decreasing our imports will be, first, to set our spindles running, swell the number of paid operators, increase their wages, thereby adding to the number and paying capacity of consumers, and thus enlarge our home market for all home products and manufactures, with prosperity in general as the result assured.

The tendency of increasing our exports and decreasing our imports will be, second, to establish a credit balance of trade for the United States. A credit balance of trade means that Europe has become our debtor, and must settle with us in money. Europe's silver money is overvalued in her gold, compared with ours, by from 3 to 7 cents on the dollar. The European merchant or banker, will, therefore, make his trade settlements with us in gold more profitably by from 3 to 7 per cent. than in his silver. And the instant that European trade settlements with the United States are made in gold, parity for our gold and silver money is established in the markets of the world.

Therewith, the 371.25 grains of pure silver in our silver dollar and the 23.22 grains of gold in our gold dollar become of exactly equal worth, as bullion, in New York.

CONTENTS.

ILLUSTRATIONS.

WILLIAM JENNINGS BRYAN.

WILLIAM JENNINGS BRYAN, statesman and presidential candidate, was born in Salem, Marion county, Illinois, March 19, 1860, son of Silas Lillard and Maria Jennings Bryan. His first American ancestor came from Ireland, and settled in the tidewater section of Virginia. It is known of this pioneer emigrant that he stood as a representative citizen of the state, and that his descendants were classed among the well-to-do families engaged in the cultivation of the soil. They took active interest in the politics of the commonwealth as Democrats, and represented their section in county and state affairs. As farmers, the Bryans of Virginia were conspicuous for industry, frugality and hospitality. They were intensely religious, and as leading members of the Baptish church were looked upon as safe advisers on the social, political and moral questions of their day. In 1752 Joseph T. Bryan left the tidewater section of Virginia and pushed westward. He located on the side of a mountain, where he found all the conditions necessary for a settler's home. From the site selected for his future dwelling, he looked down through a beautiful valley made fertile by the mountain stream that found its way to the bosom of the Rappahannock. Here he put up a log cabin after the fashion of the settlers, and fitted it for the home of his family. This house still stands as an ell to a more pretentious dwelling on the side of Oventop mountain, at the base of Marvey's Rock, the highest peak of the Blue Ridge mountains. About half a mile westward from the old homestead, on a narrow, rocky road, the Bryan meeting-house, a large, rambling structure, still stands in about the same condition as when the family of the great-great-grandfather of the presidential candidate worshipped there with his neighbors. They were hardshell, or primitive Baptists, a sect that claimed the best element of these hardy pioneer settlers, and their meeting-house was capable of seating over eight hundred worshippers, and has always been known as the Old Bryan Church. William Bryan, a son of Joseph T., died in Culpeper county in 1806, and his will, after providing for his wife, Nettie Bryan, and two maiden sisters, divided his property equally between his children, James, John, William, Aquilla, Lucy and Elizabeth. At the time of his death he was about sixty years of age. In the division of the property John, the grandfather of William Jennings, was allotted the tract of two hundred and fifteen acres near Sperryville, by reason of its location the most valuable portion of the estate. In 1807 John Bryan married Nancy Lillard, and lived in the old home place until 1826, when he sold out and removed with his family to the western borders of the State, on the Ohio river, near the mouth of the Great Kanawha. The Lillards were of Scotch origin, and neighbors of the Bryans. A remnant of the family still lived in Rappahannock and Culpeper counties at the end of the nineteenth century. They occupied positions of wealth and station in Virginia, Kentucky and Mississippi. Nancy Bryan died in 1830, and John Bryan in 1835. Their son, Silas Lillard Bryan, the father of William Jennings, removed to Missouri immediately after the death of his parents, the family having meantime scattered through several of the western states. Here he attended school, working part of the year to pay for his education, as was the custom of the time and section. After two years he removed to Marion county, Ill., where he continued his studies, and taught school for a time. He fitted himself for college, and was graduated in course, and then studied law. In 1857 he was admitted to the bar, and soon rose to prominence in his profession. He served his State as senator, superintendent of schools, judge of the circuit court for twelve years, and as a member of the State constitutional convention. The home of the Bryans was on a farm just outside the corporate limits of Salem, and the son had the advantages of the best educational training afforded by the public school of the place. He was then sent to Whipple Academy, Jacksonville, Ill., where he was prepared for college.

When seventeen years old he matriculated at Illinois college with the class of 1881. He was graduated with the highest honor and was selected as class orator. His oratorical power manifested itself when he was a mere boy, and at school he orated before admiring classmates when but eight years old, and his father encouraged the talent by allowing the boy to accompany him in his appointments at the Democratic mass meetings during the national and gubernatorial canvasses, where he listened to the celebrated orators of the section, and became greatly interested in the political questions of the day. When twelve years old he went with his father to a great Democratic demonstration at Centralia, Ill., and after listening to the most distinguished speakers of the state, he asked to be allowed to take part in the discussion. Mounting the platform in the midst of an oppressive silence, the boy could see the smile of derision that greeted his appearance. A boy, presuming to speak to the sage politicians seated on the platform, and expecting to be listened to by the thousands on the ground before him. He commenced in tones convincing and eloquent. He displayed a thorough knowledge of the questions of the current campaign, and handled the arguments with the skill of an old campaigner. His reasoning surprised them, and he soon had his audi-

ence spellbound by his eloquence. They broke the spell
as a fine turned period gave inspiration to a spontaneous
ripple of applause. With this the audience caught up the
enthusiasm of the young speaker and drowned his words
with deafening cheers, repeated as he waved them to silence
that he might continue. Cheers punctuated every sen-
tence, and when he closed there was a tremendous outburst of enthusiasm. The men came to the platform, and
lifting the boy orator on their shoulders, bore him in triumph over the heads of the audience. The orator, politician and statesman shone out in this boy of twelve years
of age, and fixed his profession. At college he was famous
not only as an orator, but as an all-round athlete. He
was one of the best baseball players, pitching as good a
ball as any man ever at the college, and as a batter could
always be depended upon to make a base hit when he came
to the bat. In field sports he was a champion and holds
at the time of his candidacy the record for the hop, skip,
and jump. His personal magnetism made him a universal
favorite while in Jacksonville, and as honor man of his
class he won the place without making an enemy. Upon
leaving Jacksonville young Bryan entered Union Law
College, Chicago, and at the same time gained admission
to the law office of Lyman Trumbull, where he took a
practical course in the business of law, at the same time
he was being initiated in the mysteries of Coke and Black-
stone. He gained two years time by this means, and
when he was admitted to the bar in 1883, he returned to
Jacksonville and opened a law office there. A ruling motive in selecting the college town was, no doubt, that it
was the scene of an acquaintance with a young lady to
whom he became attached, while each were attending
school there. This lady was Mary Elizabeth Baird, an
American girl with American ideas.

Her father was a broad-minded man, who came from Washington, Pa. Her mother was the daughter of Col. Darius Dexter, the founder of Dexterville, N. Y. They had but little capital, not even good health, and removed to the West, locating at Perry, Pike county, Ill., where Mr. Baird opened a general store, and prospered in business. Under these surroundings the daughter grew up, the constant companion of her father, who was afflicted with total blindness. The fortitude and patience of her mother taught the young girl gentleness, as she witnessed the cross she constantly bore without complaint. When fourteen years old she entered the academy at Jacksonville. It was the same year that William Jennings Bryan entered the Illinois college there. Miss Baird was selected as valedictorian of her class. The president of the academy praised her scholarship and commented on her fine mind, pronouncing her a coming woman. Upon graduating, Miss Baird returned home, and when Mr. Bryan gained his diploma at Chicago he turned his steps to the same place, and they were married and immediately made their home in Jacksonville, where she took up the study of law, while her husband commenced the practice of his profession. Mrs. Bryan was admitted to the bar, but never entered into the practice of her profession, save as an assistant to her husband. They worked and studied together, she consulting books, outlining arguments, and citing precedents. She also joined her husband in his investigations of the constantly varying conditions of political matters, and became with him thoroughly versed in the science of government, of finance and of political economy. When her mother died, her father, unable to use his eyes, became a member of her family, and she added to her duties that of reading to him the newspapers of the day, as well as the latest and most interesting books of fiction. She explained to him the changing conditions of the world, and discussed with him all the subjects read—his active mind craving such treatment. With the care of three children, with whom she daily lived, feeding, dressing and teaching them, romping with them, making herself a companion, and when they were safely asleep, then with her husband and father she would discuss law and politics, or alone she would take up Hawthorne or some other favorite American author.

Mr. Bryan's first law case was tried in 1884 in a Justice Court. It was a dispute between two farmers, involving about twenty dollars. The young attorney and counsellor as carefully prepared his case as if it were to be argued before the United States Supreme Court, and won. Entering his office with his face beaming with smiles, he shouted, "I have won my first case." Mr. Bryan attends, with his wife and family, the Presbyterian church of which he is a member and trustee. He is a member of the Young Men's Christian Association, and takes great interest in the young people in the congregation. It was a common sight in his early married life to see him with his wife and her blind father taking their way every Sunday morning to the church and in the afternoon to the Sunday-school, in which both were teachers. His devotion to his father-in-law was touching, and the busy lawyer always found time to make him less obvious of his affliction. They have three children, William Jennings, Ruth and Grace. In October, 1887, he removed to Omaha, Neb., and associated himself with A. R. Talbot, the law firm finally becoming Talbot, Bryan & Allen. The first five years he devoted entirely to the practice of his profession, and was only moderately successful in gaining pecuniary rewards, as many of his clients were impoverished farmers who could not afford to pay large fees. His affection for the poor and unfortunate forbade him to turn any such clients away, and he became known as always ready to give council and advice to the common people. Mr. Bryan's only enemies are those who disagree with him politically, and those of his own party whose jealousy has been aroused by the phenomenal rapidity of his political advancement. His integrity was never questioned. His character has never been assailed. He is known as a clean, honest man. His intense belief in the principles he advocates and his outspoken expressions of that belief has led his enemies to pronounce him a demagogue. His answer to the charges of being a Populist and pandering to the sentiment of the Socialists is, that he has never made a statement he did not believe to be true, and that he has not sought to win the approval of any class or party, that he has always been and would always remain a Democrat, but he believed the common people had rights that all parties were bound to respect. In 1891, he made up his mind that the free coinage of silver was to be the issue before the people, and since then with incidental attention to the income tax, he has concentrated his thought, energy and ability on this one subject. His first political effort was at the meeting of the Democratic state convention at Omaha, in May, 1888, to choose delegates to the national convention at St. Louis. He was a delegate, and during the absence of a committee, the waiting crowd called upon him for a speech. He devoted himself entirely to the tariff, then the absorbing issue with the Nebraska voters. His arguments were convincing, his logic unanswerable, his brilliancy and eloquence irresistible, and he carried the audience to their feet and they drowned the orator in the volume of their cheers. He had by a single speech won for the standard of "tariff for revenue only," a place in the front ranks in a Republican state, and for himself a state reputation as its champion. The very next year he declined the Democratic nomination for Lieutenant-Governor offered by the Democratic state convention, but promised the ticket his active co-operation, and he made over fifty speeches during the campaign.

In 1888 W. J. Connell, the Republican candidate for representative in congress from Mr. Bryan's district, was elected over J. Sterling Morton by 3,000 majority, although two years before the district had gone Democratic by nearly 7,000. In this campaign Mr. Bryan stumped the district for Mr. Morton. In 1890 the young men of the district took the matter in hand, and offered the nomination to Mr. Bryan, who had written the platform for the party, and best represented the young Democracy. The prospects of success were so shadowy that Mr. Bryan accepted the forlorn hope in these words: "Of course there is no show for an election, but I will make the race and do my best ; I will advocate the Democratic principle of tariff reform on every stump in the district." He was only thirty years old, and determined to put his best work in the canvass. He had a district that embraced nine counties, with a voting population of more than 72,000. The veteran politicians of the party, who controlled the party organization, took no interest in the battle, and offered no assistance in what they called a hopeless fight. They held the sinews of war, and were unwilling to loosen the purse-strings, as they saw no hope for victory. The young men took their place in the ranks under their determined leader, and made zeal and vigor take the place of campaign funds. Mr. Bryan's tour through the district became a long and continuous ovation. He issued through the Democratic committee a challenge to Mr. Connell to a joint debate on the issues of the campaign, and met him at every stand. Although Connell had served a term in the House of Representatives, and had brushed against national legislators in debate, Mr. Bryan showed himself equally familiar with the subjects discussed, and equipped with information and statistics on political and economical questions that surprised his audiences and staggered his adversary at all points. He from the outset had a marked advantage in the debate. The result of this spirited canvass was a complete surprise, as the counting of the votes disclosed a majority for Mr. Bryan of nearly 7,000. The issue was made and fought on the question of tariff reform, and on taking his seat in congress, Speaker Crisp recognized the ability of the youthful representative, and contrary to all precedent, named Mr. Bryan a member of the important committee of Ways and Means. Strange to say, this appointment was unopposed by a single member of the House. His first speech in the House of Representatives won for him immediate and marked recognition. The subject before the House was tariff reform, and as is usual with the maiden effort of every new representative, his recognition by the Speaker emptied the seats, the members taking refuge in the lobby and anti-rooms. In the midst of this confusion the young orator began. One by one, as his words rang through the chamber and penetrated the cloak-rooms, the Democratic members flocked around the new speaker, and soon, not only the Democrats, but every Republican member was in the hall, and listening intently to every word that fell from his eloquent tongue. The galleries soon filled—that secret telegraph, so potent in the national capital, had notified the visitors, and even the staid senators, that there was an unusual attraction in the House. Young Bryan held a continually increasing audience until he had finished. The interruptions interposed by experienced legislators on the Republican side, in the shape of questions that would have puzzled much older heads, but brightened the orator, and forced from him ready replies that sent one after another questioner to his seat. They had found more than their match in the youthful congressman. He aroused the enthusiasm of the Democrats, won the applause of the galleries, and disconcerted the Republicans. The first applause that interrupted his speech was when he said : "There was once a time in the history of Nebraska when there was a sheep there for every person in the state; but now if every woman in Nebraska named Mary wanted a pet lamb, they would have to go outside the state to get them." He closed this, his maiden effort in the following words :

" The country has nothing to fear from the Democratic policy upon the tariff question. It means a more equal distribution of the great advantages of this country. It means that the men who produce the wealth shall retain a larger share of it. It means that enterprise shall be employed in natural and profitable industries, not in unnatural and unprofitable industries. It means more constant employment for labor and better pay. It means the ' maximum of produce from the minimum of toil.' It means commerce with other countries and ships to carry on that commerce. It means prosperity everywhere and not by piece-meal.

" It is for this reason that young men of this country are coming to the Democratic party, as Mr. Clarkson, that high Republican authority, declared. It is because we are right, and right will triumph. The day will come, and that soon, I trust, when wiser economic politics will prevail than those to which the Republican party is wedded; when the laws in this country will be made for all and not for a few;

Mrs. W. J. Bryan.

when those who annually congregate about this capitol, seeking to use the taxing power for purposes of private gain, will have lost their occupation; when the burdens of government will be equally distributed and its blessings likewise.

" Hail that day ! When it comes, to use the language of another, ' Democracy will be King. Long live the King !' "

His graces as an orator at this time were described in the following words:

" Bryan neglects none of the accessories of oratory. Nature richly dowered him with rare grace. He is happy in attitude and pose. His gestures are on Hogarth's line of beauty. Mellifluous is the word that most aptly describes his voice. It is strong enough to be heard by thousands; it is sweet enough to charm those least inclined to music. It is so modulated as not to vex the ear with monotony, and can be stern or pathetic, fierce or gentle, serious or humorous with the varying emotions of its master. In his youth Bryan must have had a skilful teacher in elocution and must have been a docile pupil. He enriches his speeches with illustrations from the classics or from the common occurrences of everyday life with equal felicity and facility. Some passages from his orations are gems and are being used as declamations by boys at school. But his crowning gift as an orator is his evident sincerity. He is candor incarnate and thoroughly believes what he says."

In the Fifty-second Congress Mr. Bryan introduced successive petitions against the opening of the Columbian Exposition at Chicago on Sunday and also against the sale of intoxicants on the grounds. In behalf of his state he introduced bills for the erection of public buildings at Lincoln, South Omaha, and Plattsmouth. He also advocated the establishment of a United States branch mint at Omaha. In the interest of the former he introduced and supported bills placing salt, lumber, barb-wire and binding twine on the free list. In a speech of great power, and one which disclosed evidences of superior statesmanship and knowledge of constitutional law, Mr. Bryan proposed the election of United States senators by a direct vote of the people. This speech won for the youthful representative full recognition from the older members of the house, and determined his place as a leader. He was returned to the Fifty-third Congress by a scant plurality of 140 votes in a total of 30,000. This was owing to the fact that his opponent, Allen W. Field, was also an advocate of the free coinage of silver, and the canvass was turned solely on the tariff question, on which subject the sentiment in the district had greatly changed. In the Fifty-third Congress he again served on the Ways and Means Committee. He became the avowed champion of free silver, and Mr. Bland selected him as his lieutenant in the fight. In the previous Congress he had been recognized as a silver man, but his full strength and prowess was not manifested until his speech against the repeal of the Sherman silver coinage act made him an acknowledged leader. On that occasion he held the close attention of the House and of the galleries thronged with auditors for three hours. He was accorded this most respectful attention by both sides of the House and the interest of the oldest members. The scene was a remarkable one—the subject as expounded by Mr. Bryan was a revelation to conservative listeners, who had not watched the increasing interest forced upon the public mind by the demands of the yeomanry of the West and South for some relief from the burdens of a stringent money market. At the end of his second term in Congress Mr. Bryan declined a renomination, and took

MR. AND MRS. BRYAN,
FATHER AND MOTHER OF W. J. BRYAN.

up the practice of law and the lecture platform. He soon after accepted the chief-editorship of the *Omaha World-Herald*, which he made the silver organ of the Northwest. ⸸ He was presented by the Democratic members of the legislature of Nebraska as their candidate for the United States Senate in 1894, but was defeated by the Republican candidate, John M. Thurston. He then devoted his whole time to the advocacy of the free coinage of silver, both editorially and on the lecture platform throughout the West and South. He was a contesting delegate to the Democratic National Convention at Chicago in 1896, and upon the admission of his delegation to seats on the second day of the convention, he made his celebrated speech to which is accredited his nomination as their candidate for President of the United States the following day. His life from that time became a chief part in a national controversy, in which he is upholding the standard of bimetallism or gold and silver, against the standard of monometallism or gold only, as carried by Mr. McKinley.

On revisiting his old home and birthplace, immediately after his nomination, he was received by the entire populace, irrespective of party affiliations. His speech made there at that time throws a powerful light on the man, inspired by the sight of his home, the recollections of his boyhood days, the memories of his now sainted mother, at whose newly made grave he had just stood, and at whose knee he learned his duty to his God, and that patriotic father, at whose side he had imbibed the first draughts of patriotism and gained knowledge of the rights of his fellow-man. He said :

" I shall leave all discussion of party questions to those who shall follow. Returning to the scenes which surround my home, the memories of other days crowd out all thoughts of other subjects on which we may agree or differ. I remember with grateful appreciation the kindly feeling on church and party lines when I lived among you, and I shall not attempt to divide by party lines those who are here to-day.

" This is the home of my birth and early manhood. Three blocks south is my birthplace. A mile southwest is the home of my early boyhood. I shall never fail to be grateful to my parents for taking me to the farm, where I gained the physical strength that enabled me to stand the rigors of a political life.

" I believe that there is an ideal plane in politics, and I believe we stand upon it to-day. We meet to-day, recognizing the differences of feeling, but with charity toward each other. We are all imbued with the same spirit, all imbued with the same ambition, and all aiming to carry out the same purpose. We want government of the people, for the people, and by the people, and if we differ as to the means, we cannot differ as honest citizens in purpose.

" We all agree in this, that, whenever the government comes in contact with the citizen, and the citizen with the government, we all stand equal before the law. We agree that the government can be no respecter of persons, and that its strength—its matchless strength—must be the protector of the fortunes of the great and the business of the poor ; that it shall stand, an impartial arbiter, between all of its citizens.

" We believe that governments derive their just powers from the consent of the governed. We know no divine right of kings. The citizens are those upon whom rest the responsibilities of government, and while each strives in his own way to bring the government to a fit expression of the virtue of the people, we cannot agree upon those minor points which separate us.

" It was here I received my first instructions in Democracy. It was here I learned the truth of the saying that clothes do not make the man. But all who have the good of the country at heart, all these stand on a common ground, and all are citizens. These are the basic principles upon which rests the greatest nation on earth.

"I believe in the progress of the race. Talk not to me of crises through which we cannot pass, or obstacles too great to overcome. I know none such. A patriotic people are ready to meet every emergency as it arises, and as each generation follows, I believe it will be better fitted to perform the work of progress than ever before.

"It was here that I learned freedom of conscience. Every man has the right to worship God according to his own conscience, and no man shall dictate how a man shall serve his God."

BRYAN—SEWALL—PROSPERITY.

"We have come upon times of great agitation, and there are some who are quick to condemn the agitator. But, my friends, agitation in a country like ours is the only way to secure justice. The agitator is accused of stirring up discontent. Discontent lies at the bottom of all progress. If our forefathers had been content we would be to-day under British rule."—W. J. Bryan.

"When an agitator presents a question we should only inquire, Is the proposition which he presents the right one? Jefferson told us that the only duty of mankind was to protect men at the hands of their fellows. Every act beginning 'Thou shalt not' is simply an act intended to protect some individual from some other individual, and, my friends, I say to you that no government is worthy of the name which is not strong enough to protect its humblest citizen in every land from oppression."—W. J. Bryan.

Over against McKinley, the beneficiary of trusts, tariff combines and millionaire monopolists, the Democratic party has set Bryan, a man owing his advancement to his own unaided efforts, a poor man of simple life and simple associations. No clique controls him, no band of organized tax-eaters holds him in its clutch. He is not a lifelong office-holder, but has, except for two terms in Congress, been at all times self-supporting, following conjointly the occupations of lawyer and journalist. His public record in Congress shows him to have been always on the side of the people as against the classes that fatten themselves from the people's earnings. As representative his voice was raised for lower tariff duties, for an income tax, for an anti-option bill, and against the Cleveland plan for contraction of the currency.

If the single issue of free silver be set aside, the platform adopted by the Democrats in Chicago is a text-book and a creed of true Democracy. Its denunciation of the Cleveland bond-deals, its pronouncement on the tariff, its reassertion of the righteousness and propriety of the income tax, its declarations on the mooted questions of trusts and federal control of railways, its sturdy demand that the national Government shall wrest justice from the Pacific railroads, its frank utterance upon the question of a third term, and its outspoken condemnation of federal intervention in the affairs of independent States, are all expressions of traditional and militant Democracy. No earnest and sincere Democrat can repudiate such a platform to indorse the McKinley policy of plutocracy and evasion.

When Jefferson was elected, the people in the stanch Federalist sections despaired of the Republic. They expected to see the Government crumble to pieces about their ears. But to their astonishment the Republic went on, greater, more powerful and more honored than ever. And so it will go on after the election of Bryan. The historian of the twentieth century will relate the outbreak of the curious hysteria of 1896 with the same amusement with which the historian of to-day tells of the delusions of 1800.—From Editorials, N. Y. Journal.

ARTHUR SEWALL.

ARTHUR SEWALL: BIOGRAPHICAL SKETCH.

Arthur Sewall, ship builder, business man, and National Democratic candidate for Vice-President of the United States, was born in Bath, Me., Nov. 25, 1835, third son of William Dunning and Rachel Trufant Sewall. His great-grandfather, Col. Dummer Sewall, came to Bath, Me., from York, also a district of Maine, in 1762, purchased the site of the present Sewall estate, was an officer in the French and Indian war, and subsequently in the war of the American Revolution. He was fifth in descent from Henry Sewall, who was mayor of Coventry, England. Henry's grandson married Jane Dummer and emigrated to America in 1634, settling at Newbury, Mass. Judge Samuel Sewall of Salem, the first Chief-Justice immortalized by Whittier as the "good and true," who was made famous in the celebrated witchcraft trials of that town, and one of the board of overseers of Harvard, was a son of this Sewall, and his brother, John Sewall, was the direct ancestor of all the Sewalls of Maine. Arthur was educated in the best schools of Bath, and at an early age apprenticed to his father in the ship-building business. Here he passed the several grades of progression, and became a thorough master of the business. His first visit to the outside world was a voyage to Prince Edward's Island, where he exchanged a cargo of merchandise for ship timber, to supply his father's yards on the Kennebec. Upon his return, although scarcely twenty years old, he, with his brother, Edward, purchased the business of William D.

Sewall and Clark & Sewall, and, under the name of E. &
A. Sewall, launched their first ship, the *Holyhead*, of over
1,000 tons burden.   This was in 1855.

The Bath Sewalls have been closely identified with
Bath's chief industry, ship building, since 1823, when
William D. Sewall opened the small shipyard on the banks
of the Kennebec next to the family homestead.   He was
succeeded in business by Clark & Sewall.   These two
earlier firms built twenty-nine wooden vessels between
1823 and 1854.

In 1859 Mr. Sewall was married to Emma Duncan,
daughter of Charles Crooker, an old-time ship-builder and
merchant.   She was educated at Ipswich, Mass.   She has
traveled extensively, is a thorough French linguist, an
artist with pen and camera, and a historical student.   She
is a woman of quiet and refined tastes.   They have two
sons living, Harold Marsh and William Dunning, and four
grandchildren, Loyall Farragut, Arthur, Margaret and
Dorothy Sumner.

The firm of E. & A. Sewall was dissolved in 1879 by the
death of Edward Sewall.   This firm, in its twenty-four
years of existence, had built forty-six wooden vessels.   In
1879 Arthur Sewall, his son, William D. Sewall, and his
nephew, Samuel S. Sewall, a son of the late Edward
Sewall, formed the firm of Arthur Sewall & Co.

Arthur Sewall is about the only man in the country who
has persisted in building ships in the face of what other
builders have considered disaster.   Before the first administration of Mr. Cleveland grass grew in every wooden ship-
building yard on both coasts.   But Mr. Sewall, believing
that a turn for the better soon would come, resumed building,
and with greater earnestness that ever before.   There followed in quick succession four monsters, each representing
a sum beyond $125,000.   These were the *Rappahannock*,

Shenandoah, Susquehanna, and *Roanoke,* all wooden vessels, averaging about 3,000 tons net each, capable of carrying easily a tonnage in cargo of half as much more. The *Roanoke* was the largest. This ship, built in 1892, measures 3,400 tons, and is now the largest wooden ship afloat. The *Shenandoah* measures 3,258, and the *Susquehanna* 2,629. All are magnificent vessels, and as a fleet are classed superior to any other similar fleet, in one control, in the world.

In the spring of 1893 Arthur Sewall, having made a tour of all the noted shipyards of the world, to keep abreast of the march of progress in marine construction, returned to Bath and began the equipment of the firm's shipyard for the complete construction of steel sailing vessels, and the first result of this equipment was the launching of the noble steel ship appropriately call the *Dirigo.* This mammoth vessel, added to those mentioned, composed the largest fleet of sailing vessels in the United States. The *Dirigo* was launched in 1894, and measures 2,856 tons. She was the first steel sailing ship built in America. To show in what proportion the business of the Sewall's has grown in comparison with the growth of other large businesses of the country, it may be stated that the tonnage of the *Indiana,* launched in 1876, is 1,488, while that of the *Roanoke,* launched seventeen years later, is 3,400, nearly two-and-a-half times as great. In addition to his large fleet of square rigged "deep water" ships, Mr. Sewall has constructed and manages a large fleet of three and four-masted schooners, which are engaged in the coal, ice and lumber trade on the Atlantic coast. One of these vessels, the *Carrie A. Lane,* a three-masted schooner of less than 800 tons, was sent some years ago around Cape Horn from New York to San Francisco. She was the first vessel of anything like her kind or size to make this voyage.

Besides his extensive interests in shipping, Mr. Sewall is interested in railroads, the Bath Iron Works, which built the United States gunboats *Castine* and *Machias* and the ram *Katahdin*, and other enterprises. If Mr. Sewall could have had his way, and had the conditions been favorable, he would have devoted all his time to the building of ships. His capabilities as a man of affairs have been the means of drafting him into other work. His father had been a director on the Portland and Kennebec railroad, and Arthur took his father's place. He has had extensive connection with other roads, not only in Maine, but in Mexico and the Western States, and he has been president of the Maine Central system. He is a man of executive capacity, excellent business judgment and a good counsellor in business enterprises, and it is perhaps due more to his possession of these qualities than to the ownership of any very large amounts of stock that he has been called to the corporate positions which he has filled. Mr. Sewall is a Mason, and a member of the Swedenborgian church. He belongs to no other society, secret or otherwise. He is president of the Merchant's Marine Association, which has been organized to restore American shipping by discriminating duties.

He supported the navigation laws with these arguments: " If for no other reason than keeping our flag afloat, the present navigation laws merit the support of every American citizen. Why, it seems to me that it ought to be worth millions to us to have our flag carried around the world. From the patriotic standpoint, aside from that of commercial expediency, I cannot see how the thought of an American flag flying over anything that is not American can fail to be offensive. No matter what kind of a bill is passed by the friends of the so-called ' Free Ship laws,' owners will put their ships under whichever flag best suit their purposes, and so, in case of war, the advantages will be wholly on the side of the foreign owner."

During the greater part of Mr. Cleveland's first administration Mr. Sewall was on terms of close intimacy with the President, and every appointment which he recommended was made. But the free silver views of Mr. Sewall had at that time caused him to be classed by many of his friends in the East as a man who had gone wild on money questions. As a result of Mr. Cleveland's opposition to silver, Mr. Sewall fought against his renomination. He worked unceasingly for Cleveland's defeat at Chicago, standing for David B. Hill to the end but then came into line and helped elect the nominee. He never ceased to be an active member of the party. He was the unanimous choice of his party in Maine for United States Senator in 1892, and the attempt to turn him down at the State Convention by a resolution denouncing his free silver views failed.

Mr. Sewell was a delegate to the National Democratic Convention at Baltimore in 1872; at Cincinnati in 1880 and 1884; at St. Louis in 1888; and at Chicago in 1892 and 1896. At Chicago in July, 1896, he was one of the few advocates from New England of the free and unlimited coinage of silver. He was selected by the convention as their candidate for the office of Vice-president of the United States, and in an interview at the time voiced his sentiments on the platform as follows:

"There are thousands of business men in the East who are turning away from the single gold standard. It is not a class issue. In my opinion there is not a legitimate business in this country but that would be benefited by the restoration of silver to its rightful place in our national currency.

"I have been an advocate of silver ever since Congress

demonetized that metal in 1873.   I held at the time that
a mistake had been made, and have had no reason since
to change my mind.

"There are two sides to every question, and as an individual banker I have a perfect right to take a position
opposite to those who constitute the majority in the banking business.   As I said before, this is not a technical
question nor a class issue."

Upon his return to his home in Bath he received an
ovation from his fellow citizens long to be remembered
by the staid people of that maritime town.   The mayor
warmly welcomed the nominee, and Mr. Sewall in the
course of his reply to the warm welcome, said :

"It was a great convention, yet it did not seem to me to
be a partisan one.   It seemed more like the uprising of the
people, and they seemed to be controlled by one idea,
and that idea has filled me for years.   They knew that
this country is in deep distress, that it has been in distress for years, and that the great trouble is with our
monetary system; and they believe as I believe, that there
is only one remedy.   They entertain no dishonest or dis-
honorable idea, but they demand that we be carried back
to the money of our fathers, to that monetary system
under which this government flourished for so many years,
and they believe that is the only road to prosperity."

"The keynote of the Chicago platform is found in the
Declaration of Independence.   It simply implies that wherever
the Government comes in contact with the citizen, wherever
the citizen touches the Government, that all stand upon a common level, and there shall be equal rights to all and special
privileges to no one."   William J. Bryan.

SENATOR JOHN K. JONES.

THE DEMOCRATIC NATIONAL PLATFORM.

THE DEMOCRATIC NATIONAL CONVENTION met at Chicago, Ill., on Tuesday, July 7, 1896, and by a vote of 628 ayes to 301 noes, adopted the following platform :

WE, THE DEMOCRATS OF THE UNITED STATES, in national convention assembled, do reaffirm our allegiance to those great essential principles of justice and liberty upon which our institutions are founded, and which the Democratic **DEMOCRACY STANDS** party has advocated from Jeffer- **FOR Freedom of Speech,** son's time to our own—freedom **Freedom of the Press,** of speech, freedom of the press, **Freedom of Conscience,** freedom of conscience, the pres- **and the Preservation of** ervation of personal rights, the **Personal Rights.** equality of all citizens before the law, and the faithful observance of constitutional limitations.

During all these years the Democratic party has resisted the tendency of selfish interests to the centralization of governmental power, and steadfastly maintained the integrity of the dual scheme of government established by **DEMOCRACY RESISTS** the founders of this republic of **Selfish Interests and the** republics. Under its guidance **Centralization of Govern-** and teachings the great principle **mental Power.** of local self-government has found its best expression in the maintenance of the rights of the States and in its assertion of the necessity of confining the general government to the exercise of powers granted by the constitution of the United States.

Recognizing that the money question is paramount to all others at this time, we invite attention to the fact that **DEMOCRACY INSISTS UPON Honest Money as Provided for in the Constitution through the use of both Silver and Gold, a Silver Dollar having been the Original Unit of Money Value.** the constitution names silver and gold together as the money metals of the United States, and that the first coinage law passed by congress under the constitution made the silver dollar the money unit, and admitted gold to free coinage at a ratio based upon the silver dollar unit.

We declare that the **DEMOCRACY DECLARES the Result of the Act of 1873, Demonetizing Silver without the knowledge or approval of the American People, to have been the appreciation of Gold and the General Fall in Prices.** act of 1873, demonetizing silver without the knowledge or approval of the American people, has resulted in the appreciation of gold and a corresponding fall in the prices of commodities produced by the people ; a heavy increase in the burden of taxation and of all debts, public and private ; the enrichment of the money-lending class at home and abroad, the prostration of industry and impoverishment of the people.

We are unalterably opposed to monometallism, which has locked fast the prosperity of an industrial people in the paralysis of hard times. Gold monometallism is a **DEMOCRACY OPPOSES Monometallism, a British policy, Un-American and Anti-American.** British policy, and its adoption has brought other nations into financial servitude to London. It is not only un-American, but anti-American, and it can be fastened on the United States only by the stifling of that indomitable spirit and love of liberty which proclaimed our political independence in 1776, and won it in the war of the revolution.

We demand the free and unlimited coinage of both gold

and silver at the present legal ratio of 16 to 1, without waiting for the aid or consent of any other nation. We demand that the standard silver dollar shall be a full legal tender, equally with gold, for all debts, public and private, and we favor such legislation as will prevent for the future the demonetization of any kind of legal tender money by private contract.

DEMOCRACY DEMANDS the Free and Unlimited Coinage of both SILVER and GOLD at the present legal ratio of 16 to 1, making either metal a Full Legal Tender For All Debts.

We are opposed to the policy and practice of surrendering to the holders of the obligations of the United States the option reserved by law to the government of redeeming such obligations in either silver coin or gold coin.

We are opposed to the issuing of interest - bearing bonds of the United States in time of peace, and condemn the trafficking with banking syndicates which, in exchange for bonds, and at an enormous profit to themselves, supply the federal treasury with gold to maintain the policy of gold monometallism.

DEMOCRACY CONDEMNS the trafficking with Banking Syndicates to supply the Federal Treasury with Gold, to maintain the Policy of Gold Monometallism, through the sale of Interest Bearing Bonds.

Congress alone has the power to coin and issue money, and President Jackson declared that this power could not be delegated to corporations or individuals. We, therefore, demand that the power to issue notes to circulate as money be taken from the national banks, and that all paper money shall be issued directly by the treasury department, be redeemable in coin, and receivable for all debts, public and private.

DEMOCRACY CLAIMS for Congress alone the power to Coin and Issue Money.

We hold that tariff duties should be levied for purposes of revenue, such duties to be so adjusted as to operate equally throughout the country and not discriminate between class or section ; and that taxation should be limited by the needs of the government, honestly and economically administered. We denounce, as disturbing to business, the Republican threat to restore the McKinley law, which has twice been condemned by the people in national elections, and which, enacted under the false plea of protection to home industries, proved a prolific breeder of trusts and monopolies, enriched the few at the expense of the many, restricted trade and deprived the producers of the great American staples of access to their natural markets. Until the money question is settled we are opposed to any agitation for further changes in our tariff laws, except such as are necessary to meet the deficit in revenue caused by the adverse decision of the supreme court on the income tax. But for this decision by the supreme court, there would be no deficit in the revenue under the law passed by a Democratic congress in strict pursuance of the uniform decisions of that court for nearly one hundred years, that court having in that decision sustained constitutional objections to its enactment which had previously been overruled by the ablest judges who have ever sat on that bench. We declare that it is the duty of congress to

Marginal notes:

DEMOCRACY HOLDS that Tariff Duties should be levied for purposes of Revenue Only, and limited by the needs of the Government, Honestly and Economically Administered.

DEMOCRACY DENOUNCES the McKinley law as having proved a Prolific Breeder of Trusts and monopolies, enriching the Few at the Expense of the Many.

DEMOCRACY DEMANDS from Congress the use of all Constitutional power to enact and enforce an Income Tax impartially laid, so that Wealth may bear its due proportion of the Expenses of the Government.

SENATOR ARTHUR P. GORMAN.

use all the constitutional power which remains after that decision, or which may come from its reversal by the court as it may hereafter be constituted, so that the burdens of taxation may be equally and impartially laid to the end that wealth may bear its due proportion of the expenses of the government.

DEMOCRACY ADVOCATES the Protection of American Labor by restricting the Importation of Foreign Pauper Labor to compete with it.

We hold that the most efficient way of protecting American labor is to prevent the importation of foreign pauper labor to compete with it in the home market and that the value of the home market to our American farmers and artisans is greatly reduced by a vicious monetary system which depresses the prices of their products below the cost of production, and thus deprives them of the means of purchasing the products from our home manufacturers.

DEMOCRACY CLAIMS, that the depressed prices for the products of American Farmers, due to a Vicious Monetary System, deprives them of the means of purchasing the products from our Home Manufacturers.

DEMOCRACY WARNS the people against the Absorption of the Wealth by the Few, the consolidation of Railroad Systems, the formation of Trusts and Pools as a menace to a free government, demanding a stricter control by the Federal Government.

The absorption of wealth by the few, the consolidation of our leading railroad systems and the formation of trusts and pools require a stricter control by the federal government of those arteries of commerce. We demand the enlargement of the powers of the interstate commerce commission and such restrictions, and guarantees in the control of railroads as will protect the people from robbery and oppression.

We denounce the profligate waste of the money wrung from the people by oppressive taxation and the lavish appropriations of recent Republican congresses, which have kept taxes high while the labor that pays them is unemployed and the products of the people's toil are depressed in price till they no longer repay the cost of production. We demand a return to that simplicity and economy which befits a Democratic government, and a reduction in the number of useless offices, the salaries of which drain the substance of the people.

DEMOCRACY DEPLORES the waste of Public Money, as witnessed in the Lavish Appropriations of Republican Congresses.

We denounce arbitrary interference by federal authorities in local affairs as a violation of the constitution of the United States and a crime against free institutions, and we especially object to government by injunction as a new and highly dangerous form of oppression by which federal judges in contempt of the laws of the states and rights of citizens, become at once legislators, judges and executioners, and we approve the bill passed at the last session of the United States senate and now pending in the house of representatives relative to contempts in federal courts and providing for trials by jury in certain cases of contempt.

DEMOCRACY OBJECTS to arbitrary interferences by Federal Authorities in local affairs, and to government by injunction, as highly dangerous to the Rights of Citizens to Trial by Jury.

No discrimination should be exercised by the government of the United States in favor of any of its debtors. We approve of the refusal of the Fifty-third congress to pass the Pacific railroad funding bill and denounce the efforts of the present Republican congress to enact a similar measure.

DEMOCRACY APPROVES the refusal of the Fifty-third Congress to pass the Pacific Railroad Funding bill, and deplores the efforts of the present Republican Congress to enact a similar measure.

Recognizing the just claims of deserving Union soldiers, we heartily indorse the rule of the present commissioner of pensions that no names shall be arbitrarily dropped from the pension roll, and the fact of enlistment and service should be deemed conclusive evidence against disease or disability before enlistment.

DEMOCRACY RECOGNIZES the just claims of deserving Union soldiers, and heartily endorses the rule established by a Democratic administration that no names shall be arbitrarily dropped from the pension roll.

We favor the admission of the territories of New Mexico and Arizona into the Union as states, and we favor the early admission of all the territories having the necessary population and resources to entitle them to statehood, and while they remain territories we hold that the officials appointed to administer the government of any territory, together with the District of Columbia and Alaska, should be bona fide residents of the territory or district in which the duties are to be performed. The Democratic party believes in home rule and that all public lands of the United States should be appropriated to the establishment of free homes for American citizens. We recommend that the territory of Alaska be granted a delegate in congress, and that the general land and timber laws of the United States be extended to said territory.

DEMOCRACY FAVORS the admission of New Mexico and Arizona into the Union as States, and the early admission of all Territories having the necessary population.

We extend our sympathy to the people of Cuba in their heroic struggle for liberty and independence.

We are opposed to life tenure in the public service. We favor appointments based upon merit,

DEMOCRACY EXTENDS to the people of Cuba its sympathy in their heroic Struggle for Liberty and Independence.

fixed terms of office, and such an administration of the civil service laws as will afford equal opportunities to all citizens of ascertained fitness.

We declare it to be the unwritten law of this republic, established by custom and usage of one hundred years and sanctioned by the examples of the greatest and wisest of those who founded and have maintained our government, that no man should be eligible for a third term of the presidential office.

DEMOCRACY DECLARES that no man should be eligible for a Third Term of the Presidential Office.

The federal government should care for and improve the Mississippi river and other great waterways of the republic, so as to secure for the interior states easy and cheap transportation to tidewater. When any waterway of the republic is of sufficient importance to demand aid of the government, such aid should be extended upon a definite plan of continuous work until permanent improvement is secured.

DEMOCRACY ASKS the Federal Government to care for and improve all the Great Waterways of the Republic.

Confiding in the justice of our cause and the necessity of its success at the polls, we submit the foregoing declaration of principles and purposes to the considerate judgment of the American people. We invite the support of all citizens who approve them and who desire to have them made effective through legislation for the relief of the people and the restoration of the country's prosperity.

DEMOCRACY APPEALS to the considerate judgment of the American people in behalf of the justice of its cause, and invites the support of all citizens anxious for relief and the Restoration of Prosperity.

EDITOR JOHN R. McLEAN.

JUST WHAT THE PLATFORM IS.

Mr. Bryan's Chicago Speech in Favor of the Adoption of the Platform.

"Mr. Chairman and Gentlemen of the Convention:—I would be presumptuous, indeed, to present myself against the distinguished gentlemen to whom you have listened if this were but a measuring of ability, but this is not a contest among persons. The humblest citizen in all the land when clad in the armor of a righteous cause is stronger than the whole hosts error can bring.

"I come to speak to you in defence of a cause as holy as the cause of liberty—the cause of humanity."

"I come to speak to you in defence of a cause as holy as the cause of liberty—the cause of humanity. (Loud applause.)

"When this debate is concluded a motion will be made to lay upon the table the resolution offered in commendation of the administration, and also the resolution in condemnation of the administration. I shall object to bringing this question down to a level of persons.

"The individual is but an atom, but principles are eternal."

The individual is but an atom; he is born, he acts, he dies, but principles are eternal and this has been a contest of principles.

"Never before in the history of this country has there been witnessed such a contest as that through which we have passed. Never before in the history of American politics has a great issue been fought out, as this issue has been, by the voters themselves. On March 4, 1895, a few Democrats, most of them members of Congress, issued an address to the Democrats of the nation, asserting that the money

"The money question is the paramount issue of the hour." question was the paramount issue of the hour; asserting also the right of a majority of the Democratic party to control the position of the party on this paramount issue, and concluding with the request that all believers in free coinage of silver in the Democratic party should organize and take charge of and control the policy of the Democratic party.

Three months later, at Memphis, an organization was perfected, and the silver Democrats went forth openly and boldly and courageously proclaimed their belief, and, declaring that if successful they would crystallize in a platform the declaration which they had made. And then began the conflict, with a zeal approaching the zeal which inspired the Crusaders who followed Peter the Hermit. Our silver Democrats went forth from victory unto

"Assembled to enter up the judgment rendered by the plain people of this country." victory until they are assembled now, not to discuss, not to debate, but to enter up the judgment rendered by the plain people of this country. (Applause.)

" In this contest brother has been arrayed against brother and father against son. The warmest ties of love and acquaintance and association have been disregarded. Old leaders have been cast aside when they refused to give expression to the sentiments of those whom they would

"New leaders have sprung up to give direction to this cause of truth." lead, and new leaders have sprung up to give direction to this cause of truth. (Cheers.) Thus has the contest been waged, and we have assembled here under as binding and solemn instructions as were ever fastened upon the representatives of a people. We do not come as individuals. Why, as individuals we might have been glad to compliment the gentleman from New York (Senator Hill), but we know that the people for whom we speak would never be willing to put him in a position where he could thwart the will of the Democratic party. I say it was not a question of persons; it was a question of principle, and it is not with gladness, my friends, that we find ourselves brought into conflict with those who are now arrayed on the other side.

" The gentleman who just preceded me (Governor Russell) spoke of the old state of Massachusetts. Let me assure him that not one person in all this convention entertains the least hostility to the people of the state of Massachusetts.

"We stand here representing people who are the equals before the law of the greatest citizens of the State of Massachusetts." (Applause.) But we stand here representing people who are the equals before the law of the greatest citizens in the state of Massachusetts. (Applause.) When you come before us and tell us that we shall disturb your business interests, we reply that you have disturbed our business interests by your course. (Great applause and cheering.)

" We say to you that you have made too limited in its application the definition of ' business man.' The man

"The man who is employed for wages is as much a business man as his employer." who is employed for wages is as much a business man as his employer. The attorney in a country town is as much a business man as the corporation counsel in a great metropolis. The merchant at the cross roads store is as much a business man as the merchant of New York. The farmer who goes forth in the morning and toils all day, begins in the spring

and toils all summer, and, by the application of brains and
muscle to the natural resources of this country, creates

"**The farmer who, by** wealth, is as much a business man
the application of brain as the man who goes upon the
and muscle to the natural Board of Trade and bets upon the
resurces of the country, price of grain. The miners who
creates wealth, is as much go one thousand feet into the
a business man as the man
who goes upon the board earth, or climb two thousand feet
of trade and bets upon the upon the cliffs, and bring forth
price of grain." from their hiding places the precious metals, to be poured into the channels of trade, are
as much business men as the few financial magnates who,
in a back room, corner the money of the world.

"We come to speak for that broader class of business
men. Ah, my friends, we say not one word against those
who live upon the Atlantic coast; but those hardy pioneers
who braved all the dangers of the wilderness, who have
made the desert to blossom as the rose—those pioneers
away out there, rearing their children near to Nature's
heart, where they can mingle their voices with the voices
of the birds—out there where they have erected school-
houses for the education of their young, and churches
where they praise their Creator, and cemeteries where
sleep the ashes of their dead, are as deserving of the consideration of this party as any people in this country.

"**We have petitioned,** (Great applause.)
and our petitions have "It is for these that we speak.
been scorned. We have We do not come as aggressors.
entreated, and our en- Our war is not a war of conquest.
treaties have been disre-
garded. We have begged We are fighting in the defence of
and they have mocked, our homes, our families and pos-
and our calamity came." terity. We have petitioned, and
our petitions have been scorned. We have entreated, and
our entreaties have been disregarded. We have begged,

and they have mocked when our calamity came. We beg no longer; we entreat no more; we petition no more. We defy them. (Great applause.)

" The gentleman from Wisconsin has said that he fears a Robespierre. My friend, in this land of the free you need fear no tyrant who will spring up from among the people.

" What we need is an Andrew Jackson to stand as Jackson stood against the encroachments of organized wealth." What we need is an Andrew Jackson, to stand, as Jackson stood, against the encroachments of organized wealth. (Great applause.)

" They tell us that this platform was made to catch votes. We reply to them that changing conditions make new issues; that the principles upon which rests Democracy are as everlasting as the hills, but that they must be applied to new conditions as they arise. Conditions have arisen, and we are attempting to meet those conditions.

" They tell us that the income tax ought not to be brought in here, that it is a new idea. They criticise us for our criticisms of the Supreme Court of the United States. My friends, we have not criticised. We have simply called attention to what you know. If you want criticisms read the dissenting opinion of the court. That will give you criticisms. They say we passed an unconstitutional law. I deny it. The income tax was not unconstitutional when it was passed. It was not unconstitutional when it went before the Supreme Court for the first time. It did not become unconstitutional until one judge changed his mind, and we cannot be expected to know when a judge will change his mind. (Laughter.)

" When I find a man who is not willing to pay his share of the burden of the Government which protects him, I find a man who is unworthy to enjoy the blessings of a Government like ours."

" The income tax is just. It simply intends to put the bur-

dens of government justly upon the backs of the people.
I am in favor of an income tax. When I find a man who
is not willing to pay his share of the burden of the government which protects him, I find a man who is unworthy to
enjoy the blessings of a government like ours.

" He says that we are opposing the national bank currency. It is true. If you will read what Thomas Benton
said you will find that he said, that in searching history
he could find but one parallel to Andrew Jackson. That
was Cicero, who destroyed the conspiracy of Catiline to
save Rome. He did for Rome what Jackson did when
he destroyed the bank conspiracy and saved America.

" We say in our platform that we believe the right to
coin money and issue money is a
"We believe it is a function of government. We be-
function of government to lieve it. We believe it is a part of
coin money and issue sovereignty, and can no more with
money. We believe it is a safety be delegated to private in-
part of sovereignty that dividuals than we could afford to
cannot safely be delegated
to private individuals." delegate to private individuals the
power to make penal statutes or enact laws for taxation.

" Mr. Jefferson, who was once regarded as good democratic authority, seems to have differed in opinion from
the gentleman who has addressed us on the part of the
minority.

" Those who are opposed to this proposition tell us that
the issue of paper money is a function of the bank, and
"The banks ought to that the government ought to go
go out of the Government out of the banking business. I
business. stand with Jefferson rather than
with them in holding, as he did, that the issue of money
is a function of the government, and that the banks ought
to go out of the government business. (Applause.)

" They complain about the plank which declares against

the life tenure in office. They have tried to strain it to mean that which it does not mean. What we oppose in that plank is the life tenure that is being built at Washington, which excludes from participation in official benefits the humbler members of society. I cannot dwell on this longer in my limited time.

"Let me call attention to two or three great things. The gentleman from New York says that he will propose an amendment, providing that the proposed change shall not effect contracts already made. Let me remind him

"There is no intention of affecting these contracts which, according to the present laws, are payable in gold." that there is no intention of affecting those contracts which, according to the present laws, are made payable in gold. But if he means to say that we cannot change our monetary system without protecting those who have loaned money before the change was made, I want to ask him where, in law or in morals, he can find authority for not protecting the debtors when the act of 1873 was passed, when he now insists that we must protect the creditor.

"He says he will also propose an amendment to provide that if we fail to maintain a parity within a year, we will then suspend the free coinage of silver. We reply, that when we advocate a policy which we believe will be successful, we are not compelled to raise a doubt as to our own sincerity by trying to show what we will do if we fail. I ask him, if he will apply his logic to us, why he does not apply it to himself. He says that he wants this country to try to secure an international agreement. Why doesn't

" Why doesn't he tell us what he is going to do if they fail to secure an international agreement." he tell us what he is going to do if they fail to secure an international agreement? There is more reason for him to do that than for us to provide against failure. Our opponents tried for twenty years—for twenty years—to secure an international agreement. and those who are waiting for it most patiently don't want it at all. (Cheering and laughter, long continued.)

"Now, my friends, let me come to the paramount issue of the day. If they ask us why it is that we say more on the money question than we say upon the tariff question, I reply that if protection has slain its thousands, the gold standard has slain its tens of thousands. If they ask us why we did not embody all these things in our platform which we believe, we reply to them that when we have restored the money of the constitution, all other necessary reforms will be possible, and that until that is done there is no reform that can be accomplished. (Cheers.) Why is it that within three months such a change has come over the sentiments of this country? Three months ago, when it was confidently asserted that those who believe in the gold standard would frame our platform and nominate our candidates, even then the advocates of the gold standard did not think that we could elect a President, but they had good reason for the suspicion, because there is scarcely a State here to-day asking the gold standard that is not within the absolute control of the Republican party. (Loud cheering.) But note the change. Mr. McKinley was nominated at St. Louis, on a platform that declared for the maintenance of the gold standard until it should be changed into bimetallism by an international agreement. Mr. McKinley was the most popular man among the Republicans, and everybody three months ago in the Republican party prophesied his election. How is it to-day? Why, that man who used to boast that he looked like Napoleon (laughter and cheering), that man shudders to-day when he thinks that he was nominated on the anniversary of the battle of Waterloo. Not only that, but as he listens he can hear with ever increasing distinctness the sound of the waves as they beat upon the lonely shores of St. Helena. (Great applause.)

"Why this change? Ah, my friends, is not the reason evident to any one who will look at the matter? It is no private character, however pure, no personal popularity, however great, that can protect from the avenging wrath of an indignant people the man who will either declare that he is in favor of fastening the gold standard upon this people, or who is willing to surrender the right of self-government and place legislative control in the hands of foreign potentates and powers. (Tremendous applause.)

"It is no private character, however pure, no personal popularity, however great, that can protect from the avenging wrath of an indignant people the man who will declare that he is either in favor of fastening the gold standard upon this people, or who is willing to surrender the right of self-government and place the legislative control in the hands of foreign potentates and powers."

" We go forth confident that we shall win. Why? Because upon the paramount issue in this campaign there is not a spot of ground upon which the enemy will dare to challenge battle. Why, if they tell us that the gold standard is a good thing, we point to their platform and tell them that their platform pledges the party to get rid of a gold standard and substitute bimetallism. (Applause.) If the gold standard is a good thing, why try to get rid of it? (Laughter and continued applause.)

"If the gold standard, and I might call your attention to the fact that some of the very people who are in this Convention to-day, and who tell you that we ought to declare in favor of international bimetallism, and thereby declare that the gold standard is wrong and the principle of bimetallism is better—these very people four months ago were open and avowed advocates of the gold standard, and told us that we could not legislate two metals together even with all the world. (Renewed applause and cheers.)

"I want to suggest this truth, that if the gold standard is a good thing we ought to declare in favor of its retention, and not in favor of abandoning it, and if the gold standard is a bad thing, why should we wait until some other nations are willing to help us to let go? (Applause.) Here is the **"Here is the line of battle. We care not upon which issue they force the fight."** line of battle:—We care not upon which issue they force the fight. We are prepared to meet them on either issue, or on both. If they tell us that the gold standard is the standard of civilization, we reply to them that this, the most enlightened of all the nations of the earth, has never declared for a gold standard, and both the parties this year are declaring against it. (Applause.) If the gold standard is the standard of civilization, why, my friends, should we not have it? So, if they come to meet us on that, we can present the history of our nation.

"More than that, we can tell them this, that they will search the pages of history in vain to find a single instance in which the common people of any land have ever declared themselves in favor of a gold standard. (Applause.)

"They can find where the holders of fixed investments have declared for a gold standard, but not where the masses have.

" Mr. Carlisle said in 1878, 'This is a struggle between the idle holders of idle capital and the struggling masses who produce the wealth and pay the taxes of the country,' and, my friends, it is simply a question that we shall decide, upon which side shall the Democratic party fight? Upon the side of the ' idle holders of idle capital,' or upon the side of ' the struggling masses?' That is the question that the party must answer first, and then it must be answered by each individual hereafter.

"**This is a struggle between the idle holders of idle capital and the struggling masses who produce the wealth and pay the taxes of the country."— Secretary Carlisle in 1878.**

" The sympathies of the Democratic party, as described by the platform, are on the side of the struggling masses who have ever been the foundation of the Democratic party. There are two ideas of government. There are those who believe that if you just legislate to make the well-to-do prosperous, their prosperity will leak through on those below. The democratic idea has been that if you legislate to make the masses prosperous, their prosperity will find its way up through every class which rests upon them. (Applause.)

"**If you legislate to make the masses prosperous their prosperity will find its way up through every class which rests upon them.**"

" You come to us and tell us that the great cities are in favor of the gold standard. I tell you the great cities rest upon these broad and fertile prairies. Burn down your cities and leave our farms, and your cities will spring up again as if by magic; but destroy our farms and the grass will grow in the streets of every city in this country. (Applause.) My friends, we shall declare that this nation is able to

"**Burn down your cities and leave our farms, and your cities will spring up again as if by magic; but destroy our farms, and the grass will grow in the streets of every city in this country.**"

legislate for its own people on every question, without
waiting for the aid or consent of any other nation on earth.
(Applause.)   Upon that issue we expect to carry every
single state in this Union. (Applause.)   I shall not slander the fair state of Massachusetts, nor the state of New
York, by saying that when its citizens are confronted with
"Is this nation able to the proposition: Is this nation
attend to its own busi- able to attend to its own business?
ness?"   —I will not slander either one by
saying that the people of those states will declare our helpless impotency as a nation to attend to our own business.

"It is the issue of 1776 over again.   Our ancestors,
when but 3,000,000, had the courage to declare their political independence of every other nation upon earth.
Shall we, their descendants, when we have grown to 70,-
000,000, declare that we are less independent than our
forefathers?   No, my friends, it will never be the judgment of this people.   (Applause.)

"Therefore, we care not upon what lines the battle is
fought. If they say bimetallism is good, but we cannot have
it until some nation helps us, we reply that, instead of having a gold standard because England has, we shall restore
bimetallism and then let England have bimetallism because
the United States has. (Applause.)   If they dare to come
out and in the open defend the gold standard as a good
thing, we shall fight them to the uttermost. Having behind
us the producing masses of this nation and the world; having behind us the commercial interests, and the laboring interests, and all the toiling masses, we shall answer their de-
"You shall not press mands for a gold standard by say-
down upon the brow of ing to them: You shall not press
labor this crown of thorns, down upon the brow of labor this
you shall not crucify man-
kind upon a cross of crown of thorns. You shall not cru-
gold." cify mankind upon a cross of gold."

Senator Stephen M. White.

MR. BRYAN NOMINATED.

Mr. Bryan was placed in nomination by Delegate Hal Lewis of Georgia, in these words:

"Mr. President and gentlemen of the convention—I did not intend to make a speech, but simply, in behalf of the Democratic party of the state of Georgia, to place in nomination as the Democratic candidate for President of the United States, a distinguished citizen, whose very name is an earnest of success, whose public record will insure Democratic victory, whose public life and public record are loved and honored by the American people. Should public office be bestowed as a reward for public service, then no man merits this reward more than he. Is public office a public trust? Then in no hands can be more safely lodged that greatest trust in the gift of the American people than in his.

"Should public office be bestowed as a reward for public service, then no man merits this reward more than he. Is public office a public trust? Then in no hands can be more safely lodged that greatest trust in the gift of the American people than in his."

"In the political storms that have swept over this country, he has stood on the field of battle among the leaders of the Democratic hosts like Saul among the Israelites, head and shoulders above all the rest. (Applause.)

"As Mr. Prentice said of the immortal Clay, so we can truthfully say of him 'that his civil reward will not yield in splendor to the brightest helmet that ever bloomed upon a warrior's brow.' He needs no speech to in-

"His civil reward will not yield in splendor to the brightest helmet that ever bloomed upon a warrior's brow."

troduce him to this convention.   He needs no encomium
to commend him to the people of the United States.
Honor him, fellow Democrats, and you will honor your-

"Honor him and you will win for yourselves the plaudits of your constituents and the blessing of posterity." selves ; nominate him, and you will reflect credit upon the party you represent ; honor him, and you will win for yourselves the plaudits of your constituents and the blessing of posterity.   I refer, fellow citizens, to the
Hon. William J. Bryan of Nebraska." (Prolonged ap-
plause and continuous cheers.)

Delegate Klutz, of North Carolina, was the first to second Mr. Bryan's nomination.   He said :

" Mr. Chairman and gentlemen of the convention—At
the behest of the yeomen Democracy of the good old
state of North Carolina, I second the nomination of the

That friend of the people, that champion of the lowly, that apostle and prophet of this great crusade for financial reform —William J. Bryan of Nebraska. (Cheers.) young giant of the West, that friend of the people, that cham- pion of the lowly, that apostle and prophet of this great crusade for financial reform—William J. Bryan of Nebraska.   (Cheers.)

He can poll every Democratic
vote in every section of this great country, that any other
candidate here named can do.   And, more than that, he
can poll more votes from persons of different affiliations,
and do more to unite the friends of free silver than all of
them put together.   (Renewed applause and cheers.)   Cyn-
ics tell us that oratory is dead; that the admiration of divine virtues is lost to our people, but this splendid ovation
that you gave to-day to William J. Bryan, the splendid
tribute that you paid to his manhood, to his oratory, to his
patriotism and to his sincerity, gives the lie to both of
those observations.   In the young prime of his great pow-

ers, known as a fearless tribune of the people, known for his advocacy of the cause of the lowly, known as the friend of free silver and as the champion of reform, eloquent as

"If he is elected, as he will be if nominated, he will be the President of all classes and of all sections of this great country of ours."

Clay, patriotic as Webster or Lincoln, if he is elected, as he will be if nominated, he will be the President of all classes and all sections of this great country of ours." (Renewed and prolonged applause and cheers.)

" The proportion of home-owning farmers is decreasing, and that of tenant farmers is increasing. This means but one thing; it means a land of landlords and tenants, and, backed by the history of every nation that has gone down, I say to you that no people can continue a free people under a free government when the great majority of its citizens are tenants of a small minority. Your system has driven the farm owner from his land and substituted the farm tenant."—W. J. Bryan.

Respect for the Supreme Court of the United States need not blind the fact that it has not always been consistent in its interpretation of the law; has not, indeed, failed to reverse its own decisions, not once or twice, but a dozen times. The Democratic plank in support of an income tax asserts no falsehood when it sets forth that the adverse decision of the court on that tax reversed "decisions of that court for nearly one hundred years, that court having in that decision sustained constitutional objections to its enactment which had previously been overruled by the ablest judges that ever sat on that bench." Though, perhaps, the most unfortunate instance of its varying moods and tempers in construing the law, the income tax decision is not the most striking one recorded in the records of the Supreme Court. It would, indeed, be futile to hope that a tribunal constantly changing in its political complexion, could maintain for a century, unbroken consistency in its adjudication of the reciprocal rights of the States and the National Government—the issue which lies at the foundation of all the differences which divide the two great parties from which its members are drawn. —Editorials, N. Y. Journal.

THE DEMONETIZATION OF SILVER A VIOLATION OF THE CONSTITU= TIONAL CONTRACT WITH THE STATES.

Jay Cooke was the sole financial agent of the government in negotiating the original 5–20 loan of $513,000,-000, the 10–40 loan of $200,000,000, the whole of the 7–30 loan of $830,000,000 and others amounting to $2,000,-000,000, the most remarkable feat of financiering known to history. In a recent issue of the *American Magazine of Civics*, Mr. Cooke says:

"I am fully convinced that prosperity and, in fact, the very salvation of the country, depends upon a return to bimetallism and free coinage. Let us examine this silver question:

" It was not until about 1876 that the full effect of the demonetizing act of 1873 was brought to the notice of the public, and not until some time afterward, when the natural effect of this legislation began to be seen in the depreciation of silver and of all American products, that parties began to inquire more particularly into the matter. It was found that Congress had ignorantly so legislated, and the then President had ignorantly signed a bill most deadly and injurious to the welfare of all our people.

"It was freely admitted that Congress had no intention, and that the president had no intention, of demonetizing silver, when this disastrous bill was passed and signed. It is hardly necessary at this late day to present proofs of this assertion, but they are abundant. Judge William D.

Kelley said, in the House of Representatives, on March 10, 1878: ' I was chairman of the committee that reported the original bill, and aver, on my honor, that I did not know the fact that it proposed to drop the standard dollar, and did not learn that it had done it for eighteen months after the passage of the substitute offered by Mr. Hooper, when I disputed the fact.'

" I have been told, and whether the story is true or false I cannot say, that this whole action was a conspiracy upon the part of some of our own officials, who had been spending some time in London, hobnobbing with the monometallists of that city, who came home fully committed to this act of demonetization.

" When the matter was brought before Congress it was passed over lightly and carelessly, and adopted without inquiry or examination. Thenceforward, the rights which the people had enjoyed under the Constitution were refused them, and the mints of this nation were violently closed against the free coinage of silver. I have always maintained that the contract between the States and the United States has been violated by this closing of the mints to free coinage of silver, and I believe that if the question can ever be brought before the Supreme Court, it would be decided that all acts authorizing the refusal of free coinage of silver, as well as gold, would be pronounced unconstitutional.

" The act has worked infinite harm and damage to all the debtor classes, which are as fifty to one in this country, compelling all who rely upon the products of their industry to discharge their indebtedness, to pay such debts contracted when silver and gold were both equal standards of value at a time now when gold alone is recognized as the unit of value, and the basis of all value among the civilized nations of the world."

TREASURER WM. P. ST. JOHN.

MADISON SQUARE GARDEN MEET-
ING, August 12, 1896.

In the absence of Senator White, Chairman of the National Convention, Governor W. J. Stone of Missouri, at
his request, made the notification address.

Gov. Stone said in part :

"Mr Chairman : We are here this evening to give formal notice to the gentlemen nominated of their selection
by the National Democratic Convention as candidates for
President and Vice-President of the United States.

"Mr. Chairman, the convention which assembled at
Chicago on the 7th day of July last was convened in the
usual way, under a call issued in due form, by the National Democratic Committee. There was nothing out of
the ordinary in the manner of its assembling, and nothing
in the action of the committee under whose authority it
was convoked to distinguish it from its predecessors. It
was in all respects a regular national convention of the
Democratic party. Every state and territory in the
Union, from Maine to Alaska, was represented by a full
A more intelligent and quota of delegates, and I may add
thoroughly representa- with perfect truth that a more in-
tive body of Democrats telligent and thoroughly represen-
was never assembled upon tative body of Democrats was nev-
the American Continent. er assembled upon the American
continent. (Applause).

"The convention was called for two purposes : First,
to formulate a platform declaratory of party principles,

75

and, secondly, to nominate candidates for President and Vice-President of the United States. Both the purposes were fully accomplished, and accomplished according to the usages that have been recognized and the methods of procedure which have obtained in Democratic conventions for fifty years. The acts of the convention, therefore, were the acts of the Democratic party. Its work was done under the sovereign authority of the national organization, and that work was the direct outgrowth of the calm, well-matured judgment of the people themselves, deliberately expressed through their representatives chosen from among the wisest, most trusted and patriotic of their fellow-citizens in all the States. (Cries, "That's so.")

"I desire to say that although the tariff was made the issue of 1892, there were thousands of Democrats who

A Reform In our Monetary System is of far greater importance than a Reform in our Revenue Policy.

then believed that a reform in our monetary system was of far greater importance than a reform in our revenue policy. I was among those who so believed.

"Those holding to that belief did not in any degree underestimate the importance of the tariff issue—on the contrary, its importance was fully appreciated—but they believed nevertheless that the control of our fiscal affairs by a mercenary combination of Wall street bankers, dominated by foreign influences, was more perilous to national safety and more pernicious in its effect on national prosperity than all the tariffs the miserly hand of gluttonous greed could write. (Cheers.)

"However, we acquiesced in the decision of our party convention, accepted the issue as made, and as one man rallied with loyalty and alacrity to the standard of revenue reform. We rejoiced in Mr. Cleveland's election, and confidently expected, as we had a right to, that he would bring the tariff question to a speedy settlement, and strip monopoly of its opportunity to plunder the people.

" But in this just expectation we were doomed to disappointment. Instead of devoting himself to a prompt and wise solution of the important issue upon which he was elected, he incontinently thrust it aside, and began, almost at the threshold of his administration, to exercise the great powers of his office to commit the country to a financial system inaugurated by the Republican party, and which the Democratic party had time and again condemned in both state and national conventions.

The Republican Convention declared for Foreign Supremacy—for American subserviency. " The Republican convention declared for foreign supremacy— for American subserviency. It upheld the British policy of a single gold standard, fraudulently fastened upon this country, and declared that we are utterly incapable of maintaining an independent policy of our own. (Cries of "No.")

" Confessing that the gold standard is fraught with evil to our people, and that bimetallism is best for this nation and for the world, it yet declared that we are helpless, that we must stand idle while our industries are prostrated and our people ruined, until England shall consent for us to lift our hands in our own defense. To this low state has Mammon brought the great party of the immortal Lincoln.

" Upon the Republican party the hand of Marcus Aurelius Hanna has buckled a golden mail, and sent it forth dedicated to the service of plutocracy in this free land of ours. But in the Democratic party, thank God, the people were triumphant. There the clutch of the money power, after a tremendous conflict, was broken. (Applause.)

" The priests of Mammon were scourged from the temple, and to-day, under the providence of high heaven, the old party, rejuvenated, stands forth, stronger and better than ever, the undaunted champion of constitutional liberty, popular rights and national independence. (Cheers.)

" The man who holds up to opprobrium such men as constituted the Chicago Convention, who denounces them as cranks, Anarchists, or Socialists, or who in any respect impugns their intelligence or patriotism, does himself most rank injustice if he be not a knave, a slanderer, or a fool. (Prolonged applause.)

" That convention did indeed represent the masses of the people—the great industrial and producing masses of the people. It represented the men who plough and plant, who fatten herds, who toil in shops, who fell forests, and who delve in mines.

" They did not go to Wall street for their principles, nor over the sea for their inspiration. Their principles were inherited from the fathers, and their inspiration sprang from an unconquerable love of country and of home. (Applause.)

" For a leader they chose one of their own, a plain man of the people. His whole life and life work identify him, in sympathy and interest, with those who represent the great industrial forces of the country. Among them he was born and reared, and has lived and wrought all the days of his life. To their cause he has devoted all the splendid powers with which God endowed him. He has been their constant and fearless champion. They know him and they trust him. (Loud cheering.)

" Suave, yet firm; gentle, yet dauntless; warm-hearted, yet deliberate; confident and self-poised, but without vanity; learned in books and statecraft, but without pedantry or pretense; a superb orator, yet a man of the greatest caution and method; equipped with large experience in public affairs, true to his convictions, true to him-

William J. Bryan is a model American gentleman, and a peerless leader of the people. self and false to no man, William J. Bryan is a model American gentleman, and a peerless leader of the people. (Tremendous cheering.)

"Mr. Bryan, I esteem it a great honor, as it is most certainly a pleasure, to be made the instrument of informing you, as I now do, that you were nominated for the office of President of the United States by the Democratic National Convention, which assembled in Chicago in July last. I hand you this formal notice of your nomination, accompanied by a copy of the platform adopted by the convention, and upon that platform I have the honor to request your acceptance of the nomination tendered. (Applause.)

"You are the candidate of the Democratic party, but you are more than that. You are the candidate of all the people, without regard to party, who believe in the purposes your election is intended to accomplish. (Cheers.)

"May God's blessing attend you and His omnipotent hand crown you with success."

The official written notification, prepared by Senator White and handed to Mr. Bryan by Gov. Stone, says among other things:

"The National Democratic Convention, which convened in Chicago on July 7th, nominated you for the Presidency of the United States, and we, as members of the Notification Committee, appointed by that convention, are here to officially inform you of the action thus taken. While you are a Democrat and have, during your political career, been an ardent advocate of Democratic principles, you are now the official head of an organization, comprising not only those who have hitherto been Democrats, but also including within its membership numerous other patriotic Americans who have abandoned their former partisan associations, finding in our platform and candidates a policy and leadership adequate to save the Republic from impending dangers.

"We are convinced that victory awaits the people and their just cause, and assure you of the earnest support of an overwhelming majority of your fellow citizens."

To Mr. Sewall, candidate for Vice-President, the official address of notification said:

"You have proven your fealty to Democracy under most trying conditions. Residing in a community intensely Republican, with no hope of political preferment and asking no favors from an adverse dominant majority, you have loyally sustained your position and have never hesitated to profess the doctrines of a faithful Democratic. Upon the absorbing financial issue as presented by our convention, you have been sound when the hours of triumph seemed remote, and when arrogant money changers throughout the world, boasted that the conquest of the American masses was complete."

"I believe that the gold standard is made up of more misery for the human race than wars and pestilences and famines, more misery than human mind can conceive or human tongue can tell, and I shall cry out against it as long as God gives me the voice to speak."—W. J. Bryan.

THE FULL TEXT OF MR. BRYAN'S GREAT SPEECH

At Madison Square Garden, August 12, 1896—A Calm, Logical and Forcible Presentation of the Democratic Argument.

Mr. Bryan, in Accepting the Nomination for the Presidency, said :

Mr. Chairman, Gentlemen of the Committee and Fellow-Citizens : I shall, at a future day and in a formal letter accept the nomination which is now tendered by the Notification Committee, and I shall at that time touch upon the issues presented by the platform. It is fitting, however, that at this time, in the presence of those here assembled, I speak at some length in regard to the campaign upon which we are now entering. We do not underestimate the forces arrayed against us, nor are we unmindful of the importance of the struggle in which we are engaged; but relying for success upon the righteousness of our cause, we shall defend with all possible vigor the positions taken by our party. We are not surprised that some of our opponents in the absence of better argument, resort to abusive epithets, but they may rest assured that no language, however violent, no invectives however vehement, will lead us to depart a single hair's breadth from the course marked out by the National Convention. The citizen, either public or private, who assails the character and questions the patriotism of the delegates assembled in the Chicago convention, assails the character and questions the patriotism of the millions who have arrayed themselves under the banner there raised.

It has been charged by men standing high in business and political circles that our platform is a menace to private security and public safety; and it has been asserted that those whom I have the honor, for the time being, to represent, not only meditate an attack upon the rights of property, but are the foes both of social order and national honor.

Those who stand upon the Chicago platform are prepared to make known and to defend every motive which influences them, every purpose which animates them, and every hope which inspires them. Those who stand upon the Chicago platform are prepared to make known and to defend every motive which influences them, every purpose which animates them, and every hope which inspires them.

They understand the genius of our institutions, they are stanch supporters of the form of government under which we live, and they build their faith upon foundations laid by the fathers.

Andrew Jackson has stated, with admirable clearness, and with an emphasis which cannot be surpassed, both the duty and the sphere of government.

He said: " Distinction in society will always exist under every just government. Equality of talents, of education or of wealth cannot be produced by human institutions. In the full enjoyment of the gifts of Heaven and the fruits of superior industry, economy and virtue, every man is equally entitled to protection by law."

We yield to none in our devotion to the doctrine just enunciated. Our campaign has not for its object the reconstruction of society. We cannot insure to the vicious the fruits of a virtuous life ; we would not invade the home of the provident in order to supply the wants of the spendthrift ; we do not propose to transfer the rewards of industry to the lap of indolence.

We would not invade the home of the provident in order to supply the wants of the spendthrift ; we do not propose to transfer the rewards of industry to the lap of indolence.

Property is and will remain the stimulus to endeavor and the compensation for toil. We believe, as asserted in the Declaration of Independence, that all men are created equal; but that does not mean that all men are or can be equal in possessions, in ability or in merit; it simply means that all shall stand equal before the law, and that government officials shall not, in making, construing or enforcing the law, discriminate between citizens.

I assert that property rights, as well as the rights of persons, are safe in the hands of the common people. Abraham Lincoln, in his message sent to Congress in December, 1861, said : "No men living are more worthy to be trusted than those who toil up from poverty ; none less inclined to take or touch aught which they have not honestly earned." I repeat his language with unqualified approval, and join with him in the warning which he added, namely : "Let them beware of surrendering a political power which they already possess, and which power if surrendered, will surely be used to close the doors of advancement against such as they, and to fix new disabilities and burdens upon them, till all of liberty shall be lost." Those who daily follow the injunction, "In the sweat of thy face shall thou eat bread," are now, as they ever have been, the bulwark of law and order—the source of our nation's greatness in time of peace, and its surest defenders in time of war. (Continued applause.)

But I have only read a part of Jackson's utterance—let me give you his conclusion : "But when the laws undertake to add to those natural and just advantages artificial distinctions—to grant titles, gratuities and exclusive privileges—to make the rich richer and the potent more powerful—the humble members of society—the farmers, mechanics and the day laborers—who have neither the time nor the means of securing like favors for themselves, have a right to complain of the injustice of their Government." Those who support the Chicago platform indorse all of the quotation from Jackson—the latter part as well as the former part.

We are not surprised to find arrayed against us those who are the beneficiaries of government favoritism—they have read our platform. Nor are we surprised to learn **We must in this campaign face the hostility of those who find a pecuniary advantage in advocating the doctrine of non-interference when great aggregations of wealth are trespassing upon the rights of individuals.** that we must in this campaign face the hostility of those who find a pecuniary advantage in advocating the doctrine of non-interference when great aggregations of wealth are trespassing upon the rights of individuals. We welcome such opposition. It is the highest indorsement which could be bestowed upon us. We are content to have the co-operation of those who desire to have the Government administered without fear or favor. It is not the wish of the general public that trusts should spring into existence and override the weaker members of society; it is not the wish of the general public that these trusts should destroy competition and then collect such tax as they will from those who are at their mercy; nor is it the fault of the general public that the instrumentalities of government have been so often prostituted to purposes of private gain.   (Applause.)

Those who stand upon the Chicago platform believe

The Government should not only avoid wrongdoing, but it should also prevent wrongdoing. that the government should not only avoid wrongdoing, but that it should also prevent wrongdoing; and they believe that the law should be enforced alike against all enemies of the public weal.   They do not excuse petit larceny, but they declare that grand larceny is equally a crime; they do not defend the occupation of the highwayman who robs the unsuspecting traveler, but they include among the transgressors those who, through the more polite and less hazardous means of legislation, appropriate to their own use the proceeds of the toil of others.

The commandment, " Thou shalt not steal," thundered from Sinai, and reiterated in the legislation of all nations, is no respecter of persons.   It must be applied to the great as well as the small; to the strong as well as the weak; to the corporate person created by law, as well as to the person of flesh and blood created by the Almighty.

No government is worthy of the name which is not able to protect from every arm uplifted for his injury the humblest citizen who lives beneath the flag. No government is worthy of the name which is not able to protect from every arm uplifted for his injury the humblest citizen who lives beneath the flag.   It follows as a necessary conclusion that vicious legislation must be remedied by the people who suffer from the effects of such legislation, and not by those who enjoy its benefits.

The Chicago platform has been condemned by some,

because it dissents from an opinion rendered by the supreme court declaring the income tax law unconstitutional. Our critics even go so far as to apply the name Anarchist to those who stand upon that plank of the platform. It must be remembered that we expressly recognize the binding force of that decision so long as it stands

There is in the platform no suggestion of an attempt to dispute the authority of the Supreme Court. as a part of the law of the land. There is in the platform no suggestion of an attempt to dispute the authority of the supreme court. The party is simply pledged to use "all the constitutional power which remains after that decision, or which may come from its reversal by the court as it may hereafter be constituted."

Is there any disloyalty in that pledge? For a hundred years the supreme court of the United States has sustained the principle which underlies the income tax. Some twenty years ago this same court sustained, without a dissenting voice, an income-tax law almost identical with the one recently overthrown. Has not a future court as much right to return to the judicial precedents of a century as the present court had to depart from them? When courts allow rehearings they admit that error is possible. The late decision against the income tax was rendered by a majority of one, after a rehearing.

While the money question overshadows all other questions in importance, I desire it distinctly understood that I shall offer no apology for the income-tax plank of the Chicago platform. The last income-tax law sought to apportion the burdens of government more equitably among those who enjoy the protection of the government. At present the expenses of the federal government, collected through internal revenue taxes and import duties, are especially burdensome upon the poorer classes of society.

A law which collects from some citizens more than their share of the taxes and collects from other citizens less than their share, is simply an indirect means of transferring one man's property to another man's pocket ; and, while the process may be quite satisfactory to the men who escape just taxation, it can never be satisfactory to those who are overburdened.

A law which collects from some citizens more than their share of the taxes and collects from other citizens less than their share, is simply an indirect means of transferring one man's property to another man's pocket.

The last income-tax law, with its exemption provisions, when considered in connection with other methods of taxation in force, was not unjust to the possessors of large incomes, because they were not compelled to pay a total federal tax greater than their share. The income tax is not new, nor is it based upon hostility to the rich. The system is employed in several of the most important nations of Europe, and every income-tax law now upon the statute books in any land, so far as I have been able to ascertain, contains an exemption clause. While the collection of an income tax in other countries does not make it necessary for this nation to adopt the system, yet it ought to moderate the language of those who denounce the income tax as an assault upon the well-to-do.

Not only shall I refuse to apologize for the advocacy of an income-tax law by the National Convention, but I shall also refuse to apologize for the exercise by it of the right to dissent from a decision of the supreme court. In a government like ours every public official is a public servant, whether he holds office by election or by appointment, whether he serves

Every public official is a public servant, whether he holds office by election or by appointment.

for a term of years or during good behavior, and the people

have a right to criticise his official acts. "Confidence is everywhere the parent of despotism; free government exists in jealousy and not in confidence." These are the words of Thomas Jefferson, and I submit that they present a truer conception of popular government than that entertained by those who would prohibit an unfavorable comment upon a court decision. Truth will vindicate itself: only error fears free speech. No public official who conscientiously discharges his duty as he sees it will desire to deny to those whom he serves the right to discuss his official conduct.

Now let me ask you to consider the paramount question of this campaign—the money question. It is scarcely necessary to defend the principle of bimetallism. No national party during the entire history of **No National Party during the entire history of the United States has ever declared against Bimetallism.** the United States has ever declared against bimetallism, and no party in this campaign has had the temerity to oppose it. Three parties—the Democratic, Populist and Silver parties—have not only declared for bimetallism, but have outlined the specific legislation necessary to restore silver to its ancient position by the side of gold.

The Republican platform expressly declares that bimetallism is desirable when it pledges the Republican party to aid in securing it as soon as the assistance of certain foreign nations can be obtained. Those who represented the minority sentiment in the Chicago Convention opposed the free coinage of silver by the United States by independent action on the ground, that, in their judgment, it "would retard or entirely prevent the establishment of international bimetallism, to which the efforts of the government should be steadily directed." When they assert that the efforts of the government should be steadily directed toward the establishment of international bimetallism, they

The Gold standard has been weighed in the balance and found wanting. condemned monometallism. The gold standard had been weighed in the balance and found wanting. Take from it the powerful support of the money-owning and the money-changing classes and it cannot stand for one day in any nation in the world. It was fastened upon the United States without discussion before the people, and its friends have never yet been willing to risk a verdict before the voters upon that issue. (Applause.)

There can be no sympathy or co-operation between the advocates of a universal gold standard and the advocates

Between Bimetallism— whether independent or international — and the Gold Standard there is an impassable gulf. of bimetallism. Between bimetallism—whether independent or international—and the gold standard, there is an impassable gulf. Is this quadrennial agitation in favor of international bimetallism conducted in good faith, or do our opponents really desire to maintain the gold standard permanently? Are they willing to confess the superiority of a double standard when joined in by the leading nations of the world, or do they still insist that gold is the only metal suitable for standard money among civilized nations?

If they are in fact desirous of securing bimetallism, we may expect them to point out the evils of a gold standard and defend bimetallism as a system. If, on the other hand, they are bending their energies toward the permanent establishment of a gold standard under cover of a declaration in favor of international bimetallism, I am justified

Honest Money canot be expected at the hands of those who deal dishonestly with the American people. in suggesting that honest money cannot be expected at the hands of those who deal dishonestly with the American people.

What is the test of honesty in money? It must certainly be found in the purchasing power of the dollar. An absolutely honest dollar would not vary in its general purchasing power. It would be absolutely stable when measured by average prices. A dollar which increases in purchasing power is just as dishonest as a dollar which decreases in purchasing power. (Applause.)

A dollar which increases in purchasing power is just as dishonest as a dollar which decreases in purchasing power.

Prof. Laughlin, now of the University of Chicago, and one of the highest gold-standard authorities, in his work on bimetallism not only admits that gold does not remain absolutely stable in value, but expressly asserts " that there is no such thing as a standard of value for future payments, either in gold or silver, which remains absolutely invariable." He even suggests that a multiple standard, wherein the unit is " based upon the selling prices of a number of articles of general consumption," would be a more just standard than either gold or silver, or both, because "a long-time contract would thereby be paid at its maturity by the same purchasing power as was given in the beginning."

It cannot be successfully claimed that monometallism or bimetallism, or any other system, gives an absolutely just standard of value. Under both monometallism and bimetallism the government fixes the weight and fineness of the dollar, invests it with legal-tender qualities, and then opens the mints to its unrestricted coinage, leaving the purchasing power of the dollar to be determined by the number of dollars. Bimetallism is better than monometallism, not because it gives us a perfect dollar—that is, a dollar absolutely

Bimetallism is better than monometallism, because it makes a nearer approach to stability, to honesty, to justice, than a gold standard possibly can.

unvarying in its general purchasing power, but because it makes a nearer approach to stability, to honesty, to just-ice, than a gold standard possibly can.

Prior to 1873, when there were enough open mints to permit all the gold and silver available for coinage to find entrance into the world's volume of standard money, the United States might have maintained a gold standard with less injury to the people of this country ; but now, when each step toward a universal gold standard enhances the purchasing power of gold, depresses prices, and transfers to the pockets of the creditor class an unearned increment, the influence of this great nation must be thrown upon the side of gold unless we are prepared to accept the natural and legitimate consequences of such an act. Any legislation which lessens the world's stock of standard money in-creases the exchangeable value of the dollar ; therefore the crusade against silver must inevitably raise the pur-chasing power of money and lower the money value of all other forms of property.

Our opponents sometimes admit that it was a mistake to demonetize silver, but insist that we should submit to present conditions rather than return to the bimetallic system. They err in supposing that we have reached the end of the evil results of a gold standard ; we have not reached the end. The injury is a continuing one, and no person can say how long the world is to suffer from the attempt to make gold the only standard money.

So long as the scramble for gold continues prices must fall, and a general fall in prices is but an-other definition of hard times. The same influences which are now operating to destroy silver in the United States, will, if suc-cessful here, be turned against other silver-using countries, and each new convert to the gold standard will add to the general distress. So long as the scramble for gold continues prices must fall, and a general fall in prices is but another definition of hard times.

Our opponents, while claiming entire disinterestedness for themselves, have appealed to the selfishness of nearly every class of society. Recognizing the disposition of the individual voter to consider the effect of any proposed legislation upon himself, we present to the American people the financial policy outlined in the Chicago platform, believing that it will result in the greatest good to the greatest number.

The farmers are opposed to the gold standard because they have felt its effects. Since they sell at wholesale and buy at retail, they have lost more than they have gained by falling prices, and, besides this, they have found that certain fixed charges have not fallen at all.

Taxes have not been perceptibly decreased, although it requires more of farm products now than formerly to secure the money with which to pay taxes. Debts have not fallen. The farmer who owed $1,000 is still compelled to pay $1,000, although it may be twice as difficult as formerly to obtain the dollars with which to pay the debt. Railroad rates have not been reduced to keep pace with falling prices, and besides these items there are many more. The farmer has thus found it more and more difficult to live. Has he not a just complaint against the gold standard? (Applause.)

The wage-earners have been injured by a gold standard, and have expressed themselves upon the subject with great emphasis. The wage-earners have been injured by a gold standard, and have expressed themselves upon the subject with great emphasis. In February, 1895, a petition asking for the immediate restoration of the free and unlimited coinage of gold and silver at 16 to 1 was signed by the representatives of all, or nearly all, the leading labor organizations, and presented to Congress.

Wage-earners know that while a gold standard raises the purchasing power of the dollar, it also makes it more difficult to obtain possession of the dollar; they know that employment is less permanent, loss of work more probable, and re-employment less certain. A gold standard encourages the hoarding of money, because money is rising; it also discourages enterprise, and paralyzes industry.

On the other hand, the restoration of bimetallism will discourage hoarding, because, when prices are steady or rising, money cannot afford to lie idle in the bank vaults.

The farmers and wage-earners together constitute a considerable majority of the people of the country. The farmers and wage-earners together constitute a considerable majority of the people of the country.

Why should their interests be ignored in considering financial legislation? A monetary system which is pecuniarily advantageous to a few syndicates has far less to commend it than a system which would give hope and encouragement to those who create the nation's wealth.

Our opponents have made a special appeal to those who hold fire and life insurance policies, but these policy holders know that, since the total premiums received exceed the total losses paid, a rising standard must be of more benefit to the companies than to the policy holders.

Much solicitude has been expressed by our opponents for the depositors in savings banks. They constantly parade before these depositors the advantages of a gold standard, but these appeals will be in vain, because savings bank depositors know that under a gold standard there is increasing danger that they will lose their deposits because of the inability of the banks to collect their assets; and they still further know that, if the gold standard is to continue indefinitely, they may be compelled to withdraw their deposits in order to pay living expenses.

It is only necessary to note the increasing number of failures in order to know that a gold standard is ruinous to merchants and manufacturers. These business men do not make their profits from the people from whom they borrow money, but from the people to whom they sell their goods. If the people cannot buy, retailers cannot sell, and if retailers cannot sell, wholesale merchants and manufacturers must go into bankruptcy.

Business men do not make their profits from the people from whom they borrow money, but from the people to whom they sell their goods.

Those who hold, as a permanent investment, the stock of railroads and of other enterprises—I do not include those who speculate in stocks, or use stock holdings as a means of obtaining an inside advantage in construction contracts—are injured by a gold standard. The rising dollar destroys the earning power of these enterprises without reducing their liabilities, and, as dividends, cannot be paid until salaries and fixed charges have been satisfied, the stockholders must bear the burden of hard times.

Salaries in business occupations depend upon business conditions, and the gold standard both lessens the amount and threatens the permanency of such salaries.

Official salaries, except the salaries of those who hold office for life, must, in the long run, be adjusted to the conditions of those who pay the taxes, and if the present financial policy continues, we must expect the contest between the taxpayer and the taxeater to increase in bitterness. (Applause.)

The professional classes—in the main—derive their support from the producing classes, and can only enjoy prosperity when there is prosperity among those who create wealth.

The professional classes—in the main—derive their support from the producing classes, and can only enjoy prosperity when there is prosperity among those who create wealth.

I have not attempted to describe the effect of the gold standard upon all classes—in fact, I have only had time to mention a few—but each person will be able to apply the principles stated to his own occupation.

It must also be remembered that it is the desire of people generally to convert their earnings into real or personal property. This being true, in considering any temporary advantage which may come from a system under which the dollar rises in its purchasing power, it must not be forgotten that the dollar cannot buy more than formerly, unless property sells for less than formerly. Hence, it will be seen that a large portion of those who may find some pecuniary advantage in a gold standard, will discover that their losses exceed their gains.

It is sometimes asserted by our opponents that a bank belongs to the debtor class, but this is not true of any solvent bank. Every statement published by a solvent bank shows that the assets exceed the liabilities.

That is to say, while the bank owes a large amount of money to its depositors, it not only has enough on hand in money and notes to pay its depositors, but, in addition thereto, has enough to cover its capital and surplus. When the dollar is rising in value slowly, a bank may, by making short-time loans and taking good security, avoid loss; but when prices are falling rapidly, the bank is apt to lose more, because of bad debts, than it can gain by the increase in the purchasing power of its capital and surplus.

It must be admitted, however, that some bankers combine the business of a bond broker with the ordinary banking business, and these may make enough in the negotiation of loans to offset the losses arising in legitimate banking business. As long as human nature remains as it is there will always be danger that, unless restrained by public opinion or legal enactment, those who see a pecuniary profit for themselves in a certain condition, may yield to the temptation to bring about that condition.

Those who see a pecuniary profit for themselves in a certain condition may yield to the temptation to bring about that condition.

Jefferson has stated that one of the main duties of government is to prevent men from injuring one another, and never was that duty more important than it is to-day. (Applause.)

It is not strange that those who have made a profit by furnishing gold to the government in the hour of its extremity favor a financial policy which will keep the government dependent upon them.

I believe, however, that I speak the sentiment of the vast majority of the people of the United States when I say that a wise financial policy administered in behalf of all the people would make our government independent of any combination of financiers, foreign or domestic. (Applause.)

A wise financial policy administered in behalf of all the people would make our Government independent of any combination of financiers, foreign or domestic.

Let me say a word, now, in regard to certain persons who are pecuniarily benefited by a gold standard, and who favor it, not from a desire to trespass upon the rights of others, but because the circumstances which surround them blind them to the effect of the gold standard upon others. I shall ask you to consider the language of two gentlemen whose long public service and high standing in the party to which they belong will protect them from adverse criticism by our opponents.

In 1869 Senator Sherman said: "The contraction of the currency is a far more distressing operation than Senators suppose." In 1869 Senator Sherman said: "The contraction of the currency is a far more distressing operation than Senators suppose. Our own and other nations have gone through that operation before. It is not possible to take that voyage without the sorest distress.

" To every person, except a capitalist out of debt, or a salaried officer or annuitant, it is a period of loss, danger, lassitude of trade, fall of wages, suspension of enterprise, bankruptcy and disaster.

"It means ruin to all dealers whose debts are twice their business capital, though one-third less than their actual property. It means the fall of all agricultural production without any great reduction of taxes.

"What prudent man would dare to build a house, a railroad, a factory or a barn with this certain fact before him?" As I have said before, the salaried officer referred to must be the man whose salary is fixed for life, and not the man whose salary depends upon business conditions.

When Mr. Sherman describes contraction of the currency as disastrous to all the people except the capitalist out of debt and those who stand in a position similar to his, he is stating a truth which must be apparent to every person who will give the matter careful consideration. Mr. Sherman was at that time speaking of the contraction of the volume of paper currency, but the principle which he set forth applies if there is a contraction of the volume of the standard money of the world.

Mr. Blaine discussed the same principle in connection

with the demonetization of silver.   Speaking in the House

Mr. Blaine said: "I believe the struggle now going on in this country and other countries for a single gold standard would, if successful, produce widespread disaster in and throughout the commercial world." of Representatives on the 7th day of February, 1878, he said : " I believe the struggle now going on in this country and other countries for a single gold standard would, if successful, produce widespread disaster in and throughout the commercial world.

" The destruction of silver as money and the establishment of gold as the sole unit of value must have a ruinous effect on all forms of property, except those invested which yield a fixed return in money.   These would be enormously enhanced in value; and would gain a disproportionate and unfair advantage over every other species of property.''

Is it strange that the " holders of investments which yield a fixed return in money " can regard the destruction of silver with complacency ?

May we not expect the holders of other forms of property to protest against giving to money a " disproportionate and unfair advantage over every other species of property? "

If the relatively few whose wealth consists largely in fixed investments have a right to use the ballot to enhance the value of their investments, have not the rest of the people the right to use the ballot to protect themselves from the disastrous consequences of a rising standard?

The people who must purchase money with the products of toil, stand in a position entirely different from the position of those who own money or receive a fixed income.

The well being of the nation—aye, of civilization itself—depends upon the prosperity of the masses. The well being of the nation— aye, of civilization itself—depends upon the prosperity of the masses. What shall it profit us to have a dollar which grows more valuable every day if such a dollar lowers the standard of civilization and brings distress to the people? What shall it profit us if, in trying to raise our credit by increasing the purchasing power of our dollar, we destroy our ability to pay the debts already contracted by lowering the purchasing power of the products with which those debts must be paid?

If it is asserted, as it constantly is asserted, that the gold standard will enable us to borrow more money from **The restoration of bi-** abroad, I reply that the restora-**metallism will restore the** tion of bimetallism will restore the **proper ratio between** proper ratio between money and **money and property, and** property, and thus permit an era **thus permit an era of** of prosperity which will enable the **prosperity which will en-** **able the American people** American people to become loan-**to become loaners of mon-** ers instead of perpetual borrowers. **ey instead of perpetual** Even if we desire to borrow, how **borrowers.** long can we continue borrowing under a system which, by lowering the value of property, weakens the foundation upon which credit rests?

Even the holders of fixed investments, though they gain an advantage from the appreciation of the dollar, certainly see the injustice of the legislation which gives them this advantage over those whose incomes depend upon the value of property and products.

If the holders of fixed investments will not listen to arguments based upon justice and equity, I appeal to them to consider the interests of posterity. We do not live for ourselves alone. Our labor, our self-denial and our anxious care—all these are for those who are to come after us as much as for ourselves, but we cannot protect our children beyond the period of our lives. Let those who are now reaping advantage from a vicious financial system remember that in the years to come their own children and their children's children may, through the operation of this same system, be made to pay tribute to the descendants of those who are being wronged to-day. (Applause.)

As against the maintenance of a gold standard, either permanently or until other nations can be united for its overthrow, the Chicago platform presents a clear and emphatic demand for the immediate restoration of the free and unlimited coinage of silver and gold at the present legal ratio of 16 to 1, without waiting for the aid or consent of any other nation.

We are not asking that a new experiment be tried; we are insisting upon a return to a financial policy approved by the experience of history. We are not asking that a new experiment be tried; we are insisting upon a return to a financial policy approved by the experience of history and supported by all the prominent statesmen of our nation from the days of the first President down to 1873.

When we ask that our mints be opened to the free and unlimited coinage of silver into full legal-tender money, we are simply asking that the same mint privileges be accorded to silver that are now accorded to gold.

When we ask that this coinage be at the rate of 16 to 1 we simply ask that our gold coins and the standard silver dollar—which, be it remembered, contains the same amount of pure silver as the first silver dollar coined at our mints—retain their present weight and fineness.

The theoretical advantage of the bimetallic system is best stated by a European writer on political economy, who suggests the following illustration: A river fed from two sources is more uniform in volume than a river fed from one source—the reason being that **A river fed from two sources is more uniform in volume than a river fed from one source.** when one of the feeders is swollen the other may be low; whereas, a river which has but one feeder must rise or fall with that feeder.

So in the case of bimetallism; the volume of metallic money receives contributions from both the gold mines and the silver mines, and, therefore, varies less; and the dollar resting upon two metals, is less changeable in its purchasing power than the dollar which rests on one metal only.

If there are two kinds of money the option must rest either with the debtor or with the creditor. Assuming that their rights are equal, we must look at the interests of society in general in order to determine to which side the option should be given.

Under the bimetallic system gold and silver are linked together by law at a fixed ratio, and any person or persons owning any quantity of either metal can have the same converted into full legal-tender money.

If the creditor has the right to choose the metal in which payment shall be made, it is reasonable to suppose that he will require the debtor to pay in the dearer metal if there is any perceptible difference between the bullion values of the metals. This new demand created for the dearer metal will make that metal dearer still, while the decreased demand for the cheaper metal will make that metal cheaper still.

If, on the other hand, the debtor exercises the option, it is reasonable to suppose that he will pay in the cheaper metal if one metal is perceptibly cheaper than the other; but the demand thus created for the cheaper metal will raise its price, while the lessened demand for the dearer metal will lower its price.

In other words, when the creditor has the option, the the metals are drawn apart; whereas, when the debtor has the option the metals are held together approximately at the ratio fixed by law; provided the demand created is sufficient to absorb all of both metals presented at the mint.

Society is therefore interested in having the option exercised by the debtor. Indeed, there can be no such thing as real bimetallism unless the option is exercised by the debtor.

There can be no such thing as real bimetallism unless the option is exercised by the debtor.

The exercise of the option by the debtor compels the creditor classes whether domestic or foreign, to exert themselves to maintain the parity between gold and silver at the legal ratio, whereas they might find a profit in driving one of the metals to a premium if they could then demand the dearer metal.

The right of the debtor to choose the coin in which payment shall be made extends to obligations due from the government as well as to contracts between individuals.

A Government obligation is simply a debt due from all the people to one of the people.

A government obligation is simply a debt due from all the people to one of the people, and it is impossible to justify a policy which makes the interests of the one person who holds the obligation superior to the rights of the many who must be taxed to pay it. When, prior to 1873, silver was at a premium, it was never contended that national honor required the payment of government obligations in silver, and the Matthews resolution, adopted by Congresss in 1878, expressly asserted the right of the United States to redeem coin obligations in standard silver dollars as well as in gold coin.

"We are opposed to the policy and practice of surrendering to the holders of the obligations of the United States the options reserved by law to the Government of redeeming such obligations in either silver coin or gold coin."

Upon this subject the Chicago platform reads: "We are opposed to the policy and practice of surrendering to the holders of the obligations of the United States the options reserved by law to the government of redeeming such obligations in either silver coin or gold coin. It is constantly assumed by some that the United States notes, commonly called greenbacks, and the Treasury notes, issued under the act of 1890, are responsible for the recent drain upon the gold reserve, but this assumption is entirely without foundation. Secretary Carlisle appeared before the house committee on appropriations on Jan. 21, 1895, and I quote from the printed report of his testimony before the committee:

" Mr. Sibley—I would like to ask you (perhaps not entirely connected with the matter under discussion) what objection could there be to having the option of redeeming either in silver or gold lie with the Treasury, instead of the note holder? "

" Secretary Carlisle—If that policy had been adopted at the beginning of resumption—and I am not saying this for the purpose of criticising the action of any of my predecessors, or anybody else—but if the policy of reserving

If the policy of reserving to the Government, at the beginning of resumption, the option of redeeming in gold or silver all its paper presented, I believe it would have worked beneficially, and there would have been no trouble growing out of it. to the government, at the beginning of resumption, the option of redeeming in gold or silver all its paper presented, I believe it would have worked beneficially, and there would have been no trouble growing out of it, but the Secretaries of the Treasury from the beginning of resumption have pursued a policy of redeeming in gold or silver, at the option of the holder of the paper, and if any Secretary had afterwards attempted to change that policy, and force silver upon a man who wanted gold, or gold upon a man who wanted silver, and especially if he had made that attempt at such a critical period as we have had in the last two years, my judgment is it would have been very disastrous."

I do not agree with the Secretary that it was wise to
follow a bad precedent, but from his answer it will be seen
that the fault does not lie with the greenbacks and treasury notes, but rather with the executive officers who have
seen fit to surrender a right which should have been exercised for the protection of the interests of the people.

This executive action has already been made the excuse for the issue of more than $250,000,000 in bonds,
It is impossible to es- and it is impossible to estimate
timate the amount of the amount of bonds which may
bonds which may here- hereafter be issued if this policy is
after be issued if this continued. We are told that any
policy is continued. attempt upon the part of the government at this time to redeem its obligations in silver
would put a premium on gold, but why should it ?

The bank of France exercises the right to redeem all
bank paper in either gold or silver, and yet France main-
tains the parity between gold and silver at the ratio of
15½ to 1, and retains in circulation more silver per capita
than we do in the United States. (Applause.)

It may be further answered that our opponents have
suggested no feasible plan for avoiding the dangers which
they fear. The retirement of the greenbacks and treasury notes would not protect the Treasury, because the
same policy which now leads the Secretary of the Treasury
to redeem all government paper in gold, when gold is de-
manded, will require the redemption of all silver dollars
and silver certificates in gold if the greenbacks and treasury notes are withdrawn from circulation.

More than this, if the government should retire its
paper, and throw upon the banks the necessity of furnishing coin redemption, the banks would exercise the right
to furnish either gold or silver.

In other words, they would exercise the option, just as

the government ought to exercise it now. The govern-

The Government must either exercise the right to redeem its obligations in silver when silver is more convenient, or it must retire all the silver and silver certificates from circulation and leave nothing but gold as legal-tender money.
ment must either exercise the right to redeem its obligations in silver when silver is more convenient, or it must retire all the silver and silver certificates from circulation, and leave nothing but gold as legal-tender money.

Are our opponents willing to outline a financial system which will carry out their policy to its legitimate conclusion, or will they continue to cloak their designs in ambiguous phrases?

There is an actual necessity for bimetallism, as well as a theoretical defense of it. During the last twenty-three years legislation has been creating an additional demand for gold, and this law-created demand has resulted in increasing the purchasing power of every ounce of gold. The restoration of bimetallism in the United States will take away from gold just so much of its purchasing power as was added to it by the demonetization of silver by the United States. The silver dollar is now held up to the gold dollar by legal tender laws, and not by redemption in gold, because the standard silver dollars are not now redeemable in gold either in law or by administrative policy.

We contend that free and unlimited coinage by the United States alone will raise the bullion value of silver to its coinage value, and thus make silver bullion worth $1.29 per ounce in gold throughout the world.
We contend that free and unlimited coinage by the United States alone will raise the bullion value of silver to its coinage value, and thus make silver bullion worth $1.29 per ounce in gold throughout the world. (Loud applause.)

This proposition is in keeping with natural laws, not in defiance of them. The most clearly established law of commerce is the law of supply and demand. We recognize this law, and build our argument upon it. We apply this law to money when we say that a reduction in the volume of money will raise the purchasing power of the dollar; we also apply the law of supply and demand to silver when we say that a new demand for silver, created by law, will raise the price of silver bullion. Gold and silver are different from other commodities, in that they are limited in quantity.

Corn, wheat, manufactured products, etc., can be produced almost without limit, provided that they can be sold at a price sufficient to stimulate production, but gold and silver are called precious metals, because they are found, not produced. These metals have been the objects of anxious search as far back as history runs, yet, according to Mr. Harvey's calculation, all the gold coin in the world can be melted into a 22-foot cube, and all the silver coin in the world into a 66-foot cube.

Because gold and silver are limited, both in the quantity now on hand and in annual production, it follows that legislation can fix the ratio between them. Any purchaser who stands ready to take the entire supply of any given article at a certain price can prevent that article from falling below that price. So the government can fix the price for gold and silver by creating a demand greater than the supply.

International bimetallists believe that several nations, by entering into an agreement to coin at a fixed ratio all the gold and silver presented, can maintain the bullion value of the metals at the mint ratio. When a mint price is thus established, it regulates the bullion price, because any person desiring coin may have the bullion converted into coin at that price, and any person desiring bullion can secure it by melting the coin.

The only question upon which international bimetallists and independent bimetallists differ is: Can the United **Can the United States** States by the free and unlimited **by the free and unlimited** coinage of silver at the present **coinage of silver at the** legal ratio create a demand for **present legal ratio create** silver which, taken in connection **a demand for silver which,** with the demand already in exist- **taken in connection with** ence, will be sufficient to utilize **the demand already in ex-** all the silver that will be presented **istence, will be sufficient** at the mints ? **to utilize all the silver that** **will be presented at the** They agree in their defense of **mints ?** the bimetallic principle, and they agree in unalterable opposition to the gold standard. International bimetallists cannot complain that free coinage gives a benefit to the mine-owner, because international bimetallism gives to the owner of silver all the advantages offered by independent bimetallism at the same ratio. International bimetallists cannot accuse the advocates of free silver of being "bullion owners who desire to raise the value of their bullion," or "debtors who desire to pay their debts in cheap dollars," or "demagogues who desire to curry favor with the people." They must rest their opposition upon one ground only, namely: That the supply of silver available for coinage is too large to be utilized by the United States.

In discussing this question we must consider the capacity of our people to use silver and the quantity of silver which can come to our mints. It **Our people far surpass** must be remembered that we live **any equal number of** in a country only partially devel- **people in the world in** oped, and that our people far sur- **their power to consume** pass any equal number of people **and produce.**

in the world in their power to consume and produce. Our extensive railroad development and enormous internal commerce must also be taken into consideration.

Now, how much silver can come here? Not the coined silver of the world, because almost all of it is more valuable at this time in other lands than it will be at our mints under free coinage.

If our mints are opened to free and unlimited coinage at the present ratio, merchandise silver cannot come here, because the labor applied to it has made it worth more in the form of merchandise than it will be worth at our mints.

We cannnot even expect all of the annual product of silver, because India, China, Japan, Mexico, and all the other silver-producing countries must satisfy their annual needs from the annual product; the arts will require a large amount, and the gold-standard countries will need a considerable quantity for subsidiary coinage.

We will be required to coin only that which is not needed elsewhere; but if we stand ready to take and utilize all of it, other nations will be compelled to buy at the price which we fix. (Loud applause.)

Many fear that the opening of our mints will be followed by an enormous increase in the annual production of silver.

Silver has been used as money for thousands of years, and during all of that time the world has never suffered from an over-production.

This is conjecture. Silver has been used as money for thousands of years, and during all of that time the world has never suffered from an over - production. If, for any reason, the supply of gold or silver in the future ever exceeds the requirements of the arts and the needs of commerce, we confidently hope that the intelligence of the people will be sufficient to devise and enact any legislation necessary for the protection of the public.

It is folly to refuse to the people the money which they now need, for fear they may hereafter have more than they need. I am firmly convinced that by opening our mints to free and unlimited coinage at the present ratio we can create a demand for silver which will keep the price of silver bullion at $1.29 per ounce, measured by gold.

Some of our opponents attribute the fall in the value of silver, when measured by gold, to the fact that during the last quarter of a century the world's supply of silver has increased more rapidly than the world's supply of gold.

This argument is entirely answered by the fact that, **During the last five years, the annual production of gold has increased more rapidly than the annual production of silver.** during the last five years the annual production of gold has increased more rapidly than the annual production of s i l v e r. Since the gold price of silver has fallen more during the last five years than it ever fell in any previous five years in the history of the world, it is evident that the fall is not due to increased production.

Prices can be lowered as effectually by decreasing the demand for an article as by increasing the supply of it. Prices can be lowered as effectually by decreasing the demand for an article as by increasing the supply of it, and it seems certain that the fall in the gold price of silver is due to hostile legislation and not to natural laws.

Our opponents cannot ignore the fact that gold is now going abroad in spite of all legislation intended to prevent it, and no silver is being coined to take its place. Not only is gold going abroad now, but it must continue to go abroad as long as the present financial policy is adhered to, unless we continue to borrow from across the ocean, and even then we simply postpone the evil, because the amount borrowed, together with interest upon it, must be paid in appreciating dollars.

The American people now owe a large sum to European creditors, and falling prices have left a larger and larger margin between our net national income and our annual interest charge. There is only one way to stop increasing the flow of gold from our shores, and that is to stop falling prices. (Applause.)

There is only one way to stop increasing the flow of gold from our shores, and that is to stop falling prices.

The restoration of bimetallism will not only stop falling prices, but will—to some extent—restore prices by reducing the world's demand for gold.

If it is argued that a rise in prices lessens the value of the dollars which we pay to our creditors, I reply that, in the balancing of equities, the American people have as much right to favor a financial system which will maintain or restore prices as foreign creditors have to insist upon a financial system that will reduce prices.

But the interests of society are far superior to the interests of either debtors or creditors, and the interests of society demand a financial system which will add to the volume of the standard money of the world, and thus restore stability to prices.

Perhaps the most persistent misrepresentation that we have to meet is the charge that we are advocating the payment of debts in fifty-cent dollars. At the present time, and under present laws, a silver dollar, when melted, loses nearly half its value, but that will not be true when we again establish a mint price for silver, and leave no surplus silver upon the market to drag down the price of bullion.

Under bimetallism silver bullion will be worth as much as silver coin, just as gold bullion is now worth as much as gold coin.

Under bimetallism silver bullion will be worth as much as silver coin, just as gold bullion is now worth as much as gold coin, and we believe that a silver dollar will be worth as much as a gold dollar.

The charge of repudiation comes with poor grace from those who are seeking to add to the weight of existing debts by legislation, which makes money dearer, and who conceal their designs against the general welfare under the euphonious pretense that they are upholding public credit and national honor.

In answer to the charge that gold will go abroad, it **No gold can leave this** must be remembered that no gold **country until the owner of** can leave this country until the **the gold receives some-** owner of the gold receives some- **thing in return for it** thing in return for it which he **which he would rather** would rather have. In other **have.** words, when gold leaves the country those who formerly owned it will be benefited.

There is no process by which we can be compelled to part with our gold against our will, nor is there any process by which silver can be forced upon us without our consent. Exchanges are matters of agreement, and if silver comes to this country under free coinage it will be at the invitation of someone in this country who will give something in exchange for it. (Applause.)

Those who deny the ability of the United States to maintain the parity between gold and silver at the present legal ratio without foreign aid, point to Mexico and assert that the opening of our mints will reduce us to a silver basis and raise gold to a premium.

It is no reflection upon our sister republic to remind our people that the United States is much greater than Mexico in area, in population and in commercial strength.

It is absurd to assert that the United States is not able to do anything which Mexico has failed to accomplish. The one thing necessary in order to maintain the parity is to furnish a demand great enough to utilize all the silver which will come to the mints. That Mexico has failed to do this is not proof that the United States would also fail. (Applause.)

It is also urged that since a number of the nations have demonetized silver, nothing can be done until all of those nations restore bimetallism. This is also illogical. It is immaterial how many or how few nations have open mints, provided there are sufficient open mints to furnish a monetary demand for all the gold and silver available for coinage.

In reply to the argument that improved machinery has lessened the cost of producing silver, it is sufficient to say that the same is true of the production of gold, and yet, notwithstanding that gold has risen in value. As a matter of fact, the cost of production does not determine the value of the precious metals, except as it may affect the supply.

If, for instance, the cost of producing gold should be reduced 90 per cent. without any increase in the output, the purchasing power of an ounce of gold would not fall. So long as there is a monetary demand sufficient to take at a fixed mint price all the gold and silver produced the cost of production need not be considered.

So long as there is a monetary demand sufficient to take at a fixed mint price all the gold and silver produced the cost of production need not be considered.

It is often objected that the prices of gold and silver cannot be fixed in relation to each other, because of the variation in the relative production of the metals. This argument also overlooks the fact that, if the demand for both metals at a fixed price is greater than the supply of both, relative production becomes immaterial.

In the early part of the present century the annual production of silver was worth, at the coinage ratio, about three times as much as the annual production of gold ;

whereas, soon after 1849, the annual production of gold became worth about three times as much at the coinage ratio, as the annual production of silver ; and yet, owing to the maintenance of the bimetallic standard, these enormous changes in relative production had but a slight effect upon the relative values of the metals.

If it is asserted by our opponents that the free coinage of silver is intended only for the benefit of the mine-own-**Free coinage cannot re-** ers, it must be remembered that **store to the mine owners** free coinage cannot restore to the **any more than demoneti-** mine-owners any more than de-**zation took away.** monetization took away, and it must also be remembered that the loss which the demonetization of silver has brought to the mine-owners, is insignificant compared to the loss which this policy has brought to the rest of the people.

The restoration of silver will bring to the people generally, many times as much advantage as the mine-owners can obtain from it.   While it is not the purpose of free coinage to specially aid any particular class, yet those who believe that the restoration of silver is needed by the whole people should not be deterred because an incidental benefit will come to the mine-owner.

The erection of forts, the deepening of harbors, the improvement of rivers, the erection of public buildings—all these confer incidental benefits upon individuals and communities. and yet these incidental benefits do not deter us from making appropriations for these purposes whenever such appropriations are necessary for the public good.

The argument that a silver dollar is heavier than a gold dollar, and that, therefore, silver is less convenient to carry in large quantities, is completely answered by the silver certificate, which is as easily carried as the gold certificate or any other kind of paper money.

There are some who, while admitting the benefits of bimetallism, object to coinage at the present ratio. If any

There are no bimetallists who are earnestly endeavoring to secure it at any other ratio than 16 to 1.
are deceived by this objection, they ought to remember that there are no bimetallists who are earnestly endeavoring to secure it at any other ratio than 16 to 1.

We are opposed to any change in the ratio for two reasons : first, because a change would produce great injustice ; and second, because a change in the ratio is not necessary.   A change would produce injustice because, if effected in the manner usually suggested, it would result in an enormous contraction in the volume of standard money.

If, for instance, it was decided by international agreement to raise the ratios throughout the world to 32 to 1, the change might be effected in any one of three ways :

The silver dollar could be doubled in size, so that the new silver dollar would weigh thirty-two times as much as the present gold dollar ; or the present gold dollar could be reduced one-half in weight, so that the present silver dollar would weigh thirty-two times as much as the new gold dollar ; or the change could be made by increasing the size of the silver dollar and decreasing the size of the gold dollar until the new silver dollar would weigh thirty-two times as much as the new gold dollar.   Those who have advised a change in the ratio have usually suggested that the silver dollar be doubled.

If this change were made it would necessitate the recoinage of four billions of silver into two billions of dollars.   There would be an immediate loss of two billions of dollars either to individuals or to the government, but this would be the least of the injury.

A shrinkage of one-half in the silver money of the world

would mean a shrinkage of one-fourth in the total volume
of metallic money.   This contraction, by increasing the
value of the dollar, would virtually increase the debts of
the world billions of dollars, and decrease still more the
value of the property of the world as measured by dollars.
(Applause.)

Besides this immediate result, such a change in the
ratio would permanently decrease the annual addition to
the world's supply of money, because the annual silver
product, when coined into dollars twice as large, would
make only half as many dollars.

The people of the United States would be injured by a change in the ratio, not because they produce silver, but because they own property, and owe debts. The people of the United States
would be injured by a change in
the ratio, not because they produce silver, but because they own
property and owe debts, and they
cannot afford to thus decrease the
value of their property or increase
the burden of their debts.   (Applause.)

In 1878, Mr. Carlisle said : " Mankind will be fortuuate
indeed if the annual production of gold and silver coin
shall keep pace with the annual increase of population and
industry."   I repeat this assertion.   All of the gold and
silver annually available for coinage, when converted into
coin at the present ratio, will not, in my judgment, more
than supply our monetary needs.

In supporting the act of 1890, known as the Sherman
act, Senator Sherman, on June 5th of that year, said:

"Under the law of February, 1878, the purchase of
$2,000,000 worth of silver bullion a month has by coinage
produced annually an average of nearly $3,000,000 per
month for a period of twelve years, but this amount, in
view of the retirement of the bank notes, will not increase
our currency in proportion to our increasing population.

"If our present currency is estimated at $1,400,000,000, and our population is increasing at the ratio of 3 per cent.

"It would require $42,000,000 increased circulation each year to keep pace with the increase of population. per annum, it would require $42,000,000 increased circulation each year to keep pace with the increase of population, but as the increase of population is accompanied by a still greater ratio of increase of wealth and business, it was thought that an immediate increase of circulation might be obtained by larger purchases of silver bullion, to an amount sufficient to make good the retirement of bank notes and keep pace with the growth of population.

"Assuming that $54,000,000 a year of additional currency is needed upon this basis, that amount is provided for in this bill by the issue of Treasury notes in exchange for bullion at the market price."

If the United States then needed more than forty-two millions annually to keep pace with population and business, it now, with a larger population, needs a still greater annual addition; and the United States is only one nation among many. Our opponents make no adequate provision for the increasing monetary needs of the world. (Applause.)

In the second place, a change in the ratio is not necessary. Hostile legislation has decreased the demand for silver and lowered its price when measured by gold, while

Hostile legislation, by increasing the demand for gold, has raised the value of gold when measured by other forms of property. this same hostile legislation, by increasing the demand for gold, has raised the value of gold when measured by other forms of property.

We are told that the restoration of bimetallism would be a hardship upon those who have entered into contracts payable in gold coin, but this is a mistake. It will be easier to obtain the gold with which to meet a gold contract when most of the people can use silver, than it is now when every one is trying to secure gold.

The Chicago platform expressly declares in favor of such legislation as may be necessary to prevent, for the future, the demonetization of any kind of legal-tender money by private contract. Such contracts are objected to on the ground that they are against public policy.

No one questions the right of legislatures to fix the rate of interest which can be collected by law; there is far more reason for preventing private individuals from setting aside legal-tender law.

The money which is by law made a legal tender must in the course of ordinary business be accepted by ninety-nine out of every hundred persons. Why should the one-hundredth man be permitted to exempt himself from the general rule? (Applause.)

Special contracts have a tendency to increase the demand for a particular kind of money, and thus force it to a premium. Have not the people a right to say that a comparatively few individuals shall not be permitted to derange the financial system of the nation in order to collect a premium in case they succeed in forcing one kind of money to a premium?

There is another argument to which I ask your attention. Some of the more zealous opponents of free coinage point to the fact that thirteen months must elapse between the election and the first regular session of Congress, and assert that during that time, in case people declare themselves in favor of free coinage, all loans will be withdrawn and all mortgages foreclosed.

If these are merely prophecies indulged in by those who have forgotten the provisions of the Constitution, it will be sufficient to remind them that the President is empowered to convene Congress in extraordinary session whenever the public good requires such action. If, in November, the people by their ballots declare themselves in favor of the immediate restoration of bimetallism, the system can be inaugurated within a few months.

If, however, the assertion that loans will be withdrawn and mortgages foreclosed is made to prevent such political action as the people may believe to be necessary for the preservation of their rights, then a new and vital issue is raised.

Whenever it is necessary for the people as a whole to obtain consent from the owners of money and the changers of money before they can legislate upon financial questions, we shall have passed from a Democracy to a Plutocracy. Whenever it is necessary for the people as a whole to obtain consent from the owners of money and the changers of money before they can legislate upon financial questions, we shall have passed from a democracy to a plutocracy. But that time has not yet arrived. Threats and intimidations will be of no avail.

The people who in 1776 rejected the doctrine that kings rule by right divine will not in this generation subscribe to a doctrine that money is omnipotent.

In conclusion, permit me to say a word in regard to international bimetallism. We are not opposed to an international agreement looking to the restoration of bimetallism throughout the world. The advocates of free coinage have on all occasions shown their willingness to co-operate with other nations in the reinstatement of silver, but they are not willing to await the pleasure of other governments when immediate relief is needed by the people of the United

**Independent action of-
fers better assurance of
international bimetallism
than servile dependence
upon foreign aid.**

States, and they further believe
that independent action offers better assurance of international bimetallism than servile dependence
upon foreign aid.

For more than twenty years we have invited the assistance of European nations, but all progress in that direction of international bimetallism has been blocked by
the opposition of those who derive a pecuniary benefit
from the appreciation of gold.

How long must we wait for bimetallism to be brought
to us by those who profit by monometallism? (Applause.)

If the double standard will bring benefits to our people,
who will deny them the right to enjoy those benefits?
(Loud applause.)

If our opponents would admit the right, the ability and
the duty of our people to act for themselves on all public
questions, without the assistance and regardless of the
wishes of other nations, and then propose the remedial
legislation which they consider sufficient, we could meet
them in the field of honorable debate ; but when they assert that this nation is helpless to protect the rights of its
own citizens, we challenge them to submit the issue to a
people whose patriotism has never been appealed to in vain.

**We shall not offend
other nations when we
declare the right of the
American people to gov-
ern themselves, and, without let or hindrance
from without, decide
upon every question pre-
sented for their consid-
eration.**

We shall not offend other nations when we declare the right
of the American people to gov-
ern themselves, and without let
or hindrance from without—decide upon every question presented for their consideration. In
taking this position, we simply
maintain the dignity of seventy

million citizens who are second to none in their capacity for self-government.

The gold standard has compelled the American people to pay an ever-increasing tribute to the creditor nations of the world—a tribute which no one dares to defend. I assert that national honor requires the United States to secure justice for all its citizens as well as do justice to all its creditors. For a people like ours, blessed with natural resources of surpassing richness, to proclaim themselves impotent to frame a financial system suited to their own needs, is humiliating beyond the power of language to describe. We cannot enforce respect for our foreign policy so long as we confess ourselves unable to frame our own financial policy.

Honest differences of opinion have always existed, and ever will exist, as to the legislation best calculated to promote the public weal, but when it is seriously asserted that this nation must bow to the dictation of other nations, and accept the policies upon which they insist, the right of self-government is assailed, and until that question is settled, all other questions are insignificant.

When it is seriously asserted that this nation must bow to the dictation of other nations and accept the policies upon which they insist the right of self-government is assailed, and until that question is settled, all other questions are insignificant.

Citizens of New York : I have traveled from the center of the continent to the seaboard, that I might, in the very beginning of the campaign, bring you greeting from the people of the West and South, and assure you that their desire is not to destroy, but to build up. (Loud cheers.)

They invite you to accept the principles of a living faith rather than listen to those who preach the gospel of despair, and advise endurance of the ills you have. The advocates of free coinage believe that, in striving to secure the immediate restoration of bimetallism they are laboring in your behalf, as well as in their own behalf. A few of your people may prosper under present conditions, but the permanent welfare of New York rests upon the producers of wealth.

This great city is built upon the commerce of the nation, and must suffer if that commerce is impaired. You cannot sell unless the people have the money with which to buy, and they cannot obtain the money with which to buy unless they are able to sell their products at remunerative prices.

Production of wealth goes before the exchange of wealth; those who create must secure a profit before they have anything to share with others. Production of wealth goes before the exchange of wealth; those who create must secure a profit before they have anything to share with others. You cannot afford to join the money-changers in supporting a financial policy which, by destroying the purchasing power of the products of toil, must in the end discourage the creation of wealth.

I ask, I expect, your co-operation. It is true that a few of your financiers would fashion a **Columbia, her hands bound fast with fetters of gold and her face turned towards the East, appealing for assistance to those who live beyond the sea.** new figure—a figure representing Columbia, her hands bound fast with fetters of gold, and her face turned towards the East, appealing for assistance to those who live beyond the sea—but this figure can never express your idea of this nation. (Cheers.)

You will rather turn for inspiration to the heroic statue which guards the entrance to your city—a statue as patriotic in conception as it is colossal in proportions. (Loud cheers.)

It was the gracious gift of a sister republic, and stands upon a pedestal which was built by the American people.

That figure—Liberty enlightening the world—is emblematic of the mission of our nation among the nations of the earth. (Great applause.)

With a government which derives its powers from the consent of the governed, secures to all the people freedom of conscience, freedom of thought and freedom of speech, guarantees equal rights to all and promises special privileges to none, the United States should be an example in all that is good, and the leading spirit in every movement which has for its object the uplifting of the human race. (Cheers lasting several minutes.)

"I want the people of this country to read these statistics and understand what they mean. In ten counties of the State of Kansas the proportion of those renting their farms increased from 13.30 in 1880 to 33.25 in 1890, and 64.38 per cent. of the farms are mortgaged. Why, sir, these mortgages are held in the East, and if these manufacturing States, when their industries are infants, own themselves, and have a mortgage on us, what is going to be the result when they get full grown ?"—W. J. Bryan.

A $25,000 = A - YEAR POOL COMMIS-SIONER FOR VICE-PRESIDENT OF THE UNITED STATES.

This fall each ton of anthracite coal will cost every manufacturer, every merchant, every family $1.50 more than it cost last fall. That is, the price of anthracite coal has advanced in the past year a little more than 46 per cent. Why? Is it because the mines are becoming exhausted? Is it because the wages of miners and employees of coal railways have risen? Or because the cost of production has increased? Or because last year's price was below the price at which dealing in coal is profitable? Not at all. None of these conditions exists or has anything whatever to do with it.

The sole reason is that several men who were not getting rich fast enough and had control over the necessary mines and railways organized a trust "to decrease the output and to raise the price." In other words, they have taken the people individually by the throat and are making every one pay a part of this enormous tax.

Of course there are laws both federal and state against it. Of course there are certain instincts of humanity against it. But the Coal Trust cares nothing for such trifles as law and humanity. It pockets the profits and says: "If you don't like our prices, freeze!"

No form of extortion is more injurious to business than that which puts up the price of coal and makes steam and electric power too high to allow the rapid expansion of production in such communities as that in which Pool Commissioner Hobart resides.—*New York World*, Sept. 1, 1896.

SENATOR JOHN W. DANIEL.

In Accepting the Nomination for the Vice=Presidency, Mr. Sewall said:

" Mr. Chairman and Gentlemen of the Committee: You have given me official notice of my selection by the Democratic National Convention as its candidate for Vice-President.

"For the courteous terms of your message, and the kind personal expresions, I thank you.

" Having been present at that great convention, I can more truly estimate the honor its action has conferred.

" It was the greatest and most earnest convention in the history of our party. It was closer and more in touch with the people. The delegates were there to voice the sentiments of their constituents, the people of the party, for the people of the party, controlled and conducted that convention. (Cheers.)

" The Democracy of the country realize that all the great principles of our party are as potent and essential to the well-being of the country to-day as they have always been, and as they ever will be; but the overshadowing issue before the country, now made dominant by the distressed condition prevailing throughout the land, is the demand for reform in our existing monetary system. (Repeated cheers.)

All the great principles of our party are as potent and essential to the well-being of the country to-day as they have always been.

" Our party, and, we believe, a great majority of the American people, are convinced that the legislation of 1873 demonetizing silver was a wrong inflicted upon our country, which should and must be righted. (Applause.)

"We believe that the single gold standard has so narrowed the base of our monetary structure that it is unstable and unsafe, and so dwarfed it in its development and in its power to furnish the necessary financial blood to the nation, that commercial and industrial paralysis has followed.

"We believe that we need and must have the broad and expanding foundation of both gold and silver to support a monetary system strong and stable, capable of meeting the demands of a growing country, and an industrious, energetic and enterprising people—a system that will not be weakened and panic-stricken by every foreign draft upon us ; a system that will maintain a parity of just values and the nation's money, and protect us from the frequent fluctuations of to-day, so disastrous to every business and industry of the land.

We demand the free coinage of silver, the opening of our mints to both money metals without discrimination, the return to the money of our fathers, the money of the Constitution, gold and silver. "We demand the free coinage of silver, the opening of our mints to both money metals without discrimination, the return to the money of our fathers, the money of the Constitution, gold and silver. (Cheers.)

"We believe this is the remedy and the only remedy for the evil from which we are now suffering, the evil that is now so fast devastating and impoverishing our land and people, bringing poverty to our homes and bankruptcy to our business, which, if allowed to continue, will grow until our very institutions are threatened.

"The demonetization of silver has thrown the whole primary money function on gold, appreciating its value and purchasing power. Restore the money function to silver and silver will appreciate, and its purchasing power increase. Take from gold its monopoly, its value will be reduced, and in due course the parity of the two metals will again obtain under natural causes. (Cheers.)

" We shall then have a broad and unlimited foundation for a monetary system commensurate with our country's needs, and future development, not the unsafe basis of to-day, reduced by half by the removal of silver and continually undermined by foreigners carrying from us our gold.

This is the reform to which we are pledged, the reform the people demand, the return to the monetary system of over eighty years of our national existence. This is the reform to which we are pledged, the reform the people demand, the return to the monetary system of over eighty years of our national existence.

The Democratic party has already given its approval and its pledge. Our opponents admit the wisdom of the principle for which we contend, but ask us to await the permission and co-operation of other nations. (Cries of "No!")

"Our people will not wait. They will not ask permission of any nation on earth to relieve themselves of the cause of their distress. The issue has been made. The people stand ready to render their verdict next November. (Cheers.)

"Mr. Chairman, unequivocally and through sincere conviction I indorse the platform on which I have been nominated. (Prolonged cheering.)

"I believe we are right. The people are with us, and what the people declare to be right must always prevail. (Cheers.)

"I accept the nomination, and, with the people's confirmation, every effort of which God shall render me capable will be exerted in support of the principles involved." (Long cheering.)

GOLD BUG STATISTICS.

> these juggling fiends
> That palter with us in a double sense ;
> That keep the word of promise to our ear,
> And break it to our hope.

That these are times of great business depression and even of actual suffering, is keenly felt by all, and yet when we assert that the farmers and wage-earners of this country find it almost impossible to obtain a living, we are told by men like Atkinson, White and others, that there never was a time when wages were so high and the cost of living so cheap, and they bring forward abundant statistics to show that the farmers are doing well, and that there are fewer mortgages now than ever before.

That there are fewer mortgages is undoubtedly true, but Atkinson, White & Co., carefully conceal the true reason, which is, that a large proportion of the mortgages have been foreclosed, and the property is now in the possession of the mortgagees!

As to wages. Wages in many cases have not fallen, because the labor unions have fought against a reduction. But look at the unemployed! And in many cases an actual reduction *has* taken place.

From reports of labor commissioners, abstracts of which are given in Commissioner Wright's bi-monthly bulletin, the following extracts will show something about the " rise in wages " and the regularity and conditions of employment:

Colorado—Number of unemployed, March, 1893, 8,000; number of unemployed, August 31, 1893, 45,000.

Connecticut—Number who received poor relief in 21 towns in 1875, 998 ; in 1894, 10,792.

New Hampshire—Out of 711 individual workmen catechised, 283 reported that their earnings were less than their living expenses, 429 had received stationary wages, 211 had received decreased wages, and one had received an increase. This was for 1894.

North Carolina—Wages paid farm laborers in 1893, $9.50 per month ; in 1894, $9 ; in 1895, $8.75.

New York, 1895—Out of 695 labor organizations, 544 reported that reductions would have been forced upon them, had it not been for their unions. The unions lost $13,577,542.32 from 1885 to 1893, in strikes, lockouts, and boycotts, in gaining $10,324,588.76 in wages.

. Rhode Island—Out of 2,229 employees in textiles, 1,692 were unemployed, more or less, during the year 1894 ; 1,367 had their wages decreased, and 36 received an increase.

Massachusetts—Average wages in 4,093 establishments, 1893, $436.13 ; 1894, $421.81, a loss of $14.32.

Pennsylvania—Loss from strikes and lockouts, 1881–1894, $25,179,210 ; employees in 412 establishments, 1892, 149,690; 1893, 132,653; 1894, 116,310, a loss in two years of 33,380.

Michigan—Farm laborers who received an increase during five years ending 1894, 335 ; number suffering a decrease, 3,395.

And so it goes.

SENATOR RICHARD PARKS BLAND.

BLAND'S ESTIMATE OF BRYAN.

To the Editor of the World:

Mr. Bryan, as a candidate of the Democratic party for the Presidency, will, in my opinion, prove eminently a representative candidate for the issues now before the people, and for the political situation as it now exists.

I served two terms with him in Congress and therefore have had opportunities to estimate his worth, his ability, his zeal, his honesty and his integrity as a statesman.

I have known Mr. Bryan for several years. I served two terms with him in Congress and therefore had opportunities to estimate his worth, his ability, his zeal, his honesty and his integrity as a statesman.

There is no question that Mr. Bryan is in hearty sympathy with the Chicago platform and is earnestly desirous of victory for the purpose of securing such legislation as will carry into effect the promises there made.

Old-time politicians must understand—and if they do not now understand the future will reveal to them the fact —that we have entered upon a new era in politics in our country. For fifty years in our history the public mind has been diverted from the great economic questions. Public thought has been directed more particularly to questions growing out of the peculiar situation of the states under the Constitution, part slave and part free.

For fifty years the slavery question dominated the politics of this country. First, the effort to abolish slavery; second, the victory of the Republican party in 1860, culminating in the civil war and the abolition of slavery, and the period of reconstruction that followed. The great questions involved in this overshadowed all other issues, and it broke up the Democratic party as it existed under Jefferson, Madison, Monroe, and Jackson, to a great extent.

The new party that arrayed itself in hostility to Democracy, the Republican party, brought forth with its existence these new issues. They have been fought out and have been settled, and settled to the satisfaction of the American people, North, South, East, and West.

During this conflict against slavery it has so happened that great advantages were gained in legislation by those who watched their opportunities to secure for themselves such advantages in legislative enactments as might enrich them.

The building of the Pacific railroads, the immense land grants and subsidies to these roads, the necessity for high tariffs during the war, the necessity for the issue of bonds to carry on the war, the necessity also for the issue of legal-tender greenbacks and other war measures have been taken advantage of by the money changers of the country for their own benefit.

It would make this article too long and deviate too far from its original purpose to go into any details with reference to these matters. They are simply referred to to show that in the past certain classes in this country have had the benefit of this government. It has been run to a great extent in their interest, and the interest of these classes has been to run the government for what money they could make out of it. It is these classes of people that are to-day arrayed against the Democratic candidate, Mr. Bryan.

Since, therefore the great issues out of which the war arose have now passed away, the people are now turning their attention to economic questions, and are making every effort possible to get control of their government that they may run it for themselves and in their own interest, and not in the interest of classes.

In other words, it is an effort on the part of the people to come back to the times of Jefferson and Jackson, and to follow the doctrines laid down by those great statesmen.

Jefferson predicted the very condition in which we are to-day, should the money power monopolize and get control of the government ; hence, while the silver question is the dominant issue, and the issue around which the people are rallying, yet behind all this is still the great question : Shall the classes control this government, or shall it be controlled by the masses ?

As the representative of the masses Mr. Bryan stands pre-eminent. He is a man of the new generation. He is one among those who are entering upon the political arena, and upon whom will devolve the future battles of this country.

The politician who believes that the money question, or the silver question, is the whole issue in this campaign will find that he is much mistaken, not only as to the present, but as to the political future. In our future political history the great struggle will be on the part of the people to gain control of their own,

which is the management of the government by the
people.

Mr. Bryan is a young man of splendid attainments, of
a high order of ability, purity of character and of motives
in harmony with the masses of the people. Hence, it
may be said that in selecting him at Chicago to represent
the issues in this campaign, and the future issues of our
political history, our party has made no mistake.

That the Democratic party has made what may be
called a new departure is true On the other hand, it is
only a departure by which it has cut itself loose wholly,
absolutely and unconditionally, from all the past of which
I have spoken above, and has gone back to the beginning;
has taken up the doctrines of Jefferson and Jackson, and
of our fathers, who battled against a centralized government at Washington, and a centralization of wealth, dangerous to the welfare and liberty of the people. Upon
the lines of Jefferson and Jackson, and the old Democratic fathers, the Democratic party will make battle in
the future.

Mr. Bryan is essentially a Democrat in all that this word
implies. He is a plain, unassuming man. His sympathies
are with the masses of the plain people of this country.
In his character he may be com-
pared to Abraham Lincoln, who
looked to the welfare of plain
people as being the true object
and purpose of government. That
the people believe that he is such
a man was shown by the enthusi-
asm of the masses exhibited for him on his trip from his
home in Lincoln, Neb., to New York, for it may be said
without exaggeration that probably never before in the
history of the country was there such an exhibition of

**Mr. Bryan in his char-
acter may be compared to
Abraham Lincoln, who
looked to the welfare of
plain people as being the
true object and purpose of
government.**

enthusiastic devotion to a man and to a cause that he represents as was displayed at every station where his train
stopped.

Crowds thronged into the towns from the country, and
the people all joined together in giving him a hearty
greeting. Indeed, it looked like a mob from Lincoln to
New York, and the nearer we got to New York the larger
the mob. It was difficult to get from the train to the depots, and from depots to hotels, and from hotels to opera-
houses, such was the enthusiastic demonstration for the
candidate.

As to whether Mr. Bryan intends to make public
speeches in the future I do not know, but it may be predicted that if he enter upon a campaign of this kind, it
will be memorable in our history.
He is a young man of fine phy-
sique, great powers of endurance,
great energy, and yet with all that,
patient, affable, forbearing, and
he convinces all who come in contact with him that he is sincere
and earnest in his convictions.

No man who has been thrown
in his society as I have been both in the halls of Congress,
in private life and in public campaign, can for one moment
question this. That he is ambitious no one denies. That he
is but human, and wishes to be of service to his follow-
men, not only for the good of his own name, but for the
good of his country, I have no reason to doubt.

I think it may be said, without fear of denial, that if
Mr. Bryan is elected he will use every legitimate power
to carry out the pledges he has made to the people. His
honesty of purpose is evident. His enemies grant that ;
his friends are satisfied upon that point. The effect of his

journey from the West to the East is now seen and acknowledged by all. No one has the hardihood to dispute
that it was a grand success so far as exciting an interest
among the people in the issues involved in this campaign
is concerned. No one can deny that the immense crowds
which greeted him along the way, are evidences that the
people are with him in this campaign. Especially is this
so, since, although people may have come—and many did
come, no doubt—out of curiosity to see a man who had
been nominated for the Presidency by the dominant political party, yet those who wit-
nessed these demonstrations and
meetings did not fail to observe
that nearly all who were thus assembled, whether they numbered
500 or 5,000 or 20,000, were
shouting and cheering and giving
every evidence of their sympathy
with the man and his cause.
It has at once aroused the peo-
ple to a discussion of the issues involved, earlier and more
earnestly than they have ever been discussed in any previous campaign. This has been one of the effects of his
trip from the West to the East.

Another effect that his trip has had has been to encour-
age the friends of Democracy and to confirm them in the
opinion that they have a candidate with all the ability and
all the sincerity and physical power to lead to victory.
His demonstration in New York city, at Madison Square
Garden, was a magnificent ovation to him. The immense
throng that was admitted to the theatre and the tens of
thousands who were unable to gain admission and re-
mained outside to hear him from the hotel balcony is evidence that, so far as the laboring and producing masses

of the people are concerned, he has their confidence and their sympathy.

His speech at Madison Square Garden was an able defense, if defense it might be called, of the Chicago platform. It was more than that. It was a powerful attack, and, as I regard it, an unanswerable argument, against the single gold standard and the present condition of our finances.

It may be said that my zeal for this cause may lead me not only to overestimate the strength and character of our candidate, but also the strength of the cause he represents, yet the public man who now hesitates, and especially the Democrat who now lags behind in this great battle, will find himself not only isolated at this time, but for all time to come, as a Democrat, for it can be set down as being as certain as the future can be predicted that the old-time Democracy, which has made its battles on the slavery question and the war question and all these questions, is dead, and dead forever. And old-time leaders must comprehend this fact. When I say the party is dead I mean that it is dead as to those past issues. I do not mean to say that the Democratic party itself is dead, but, on the contrary, it has new life and new vigor, and is now on the high road, not only to victory in this campaign, but to popular favor for many, many years to come.

It may be called a resurrection of the old issues of Jefferson and Jackson, in which the people took up Democracy to do battle against plutocracy in all its forms; against the Hamilton theory of government, which meant government by the classes instead of the masses. These issues are now renewed and are to be again fought out, and the Democrat who cannot stand in the party upon these issues is right in leaving it and in going to the party of McKinley, which supports simply the old Hamiltonian theory.

As a representative of this new departure of Democracy, I know of no man who is better fitted for being a leader of the party than Mr. Bryan.

R. P. BLAND.

August 17, 1896.

WHO ARE THE DEBTORS?

The gold advocates and particularly clerical servants of Mammon, like the Rev. Dr. McArthur, to whom a call from the Lord is always most effectual when sounded through a golden trumpet and by a rich congregation, try to convey the impression that debtors are a poor, disreputable and dishonest class, constantly trying to shirk their obligations and avoid paying what they justly owe. Now, it is true that there is a certain class of debtors that may be thus characterized. They are the men who always owe small bills to their landlord, their grocer, and to friends from whom they have borrowed a dollar or two. Payment of their debts is with such men a sort of happy-go-lucky affair; if they have a streak of luck, they pay (sometimes), but they never exercise any self-denial for the sake of getting out of their debts. With such men the medium of exchange cuts no figure ; free coinage will never affect them.

Their debts are not scaled fifty cents on the dollar, but

100 cents, and yet McArthur and men of his kidney hold up such dead-beats as typical debtors.

The debtors to whom an honest dollar is of importance, and upon whom the incubus of an unjust and dishonest gold standard presses most severely, are the men who have built up the nation and made all our great improvements. They have built our railroads, our bridges, our steamships, our warehouses and colossal "sky-scrapers." They are the men who have built the homes of the people, changed wild forests into fertile fields, and fed the world. They have taken dead and idle capital, breathed into it the breath of life, and made it a living power. Without them capital would have been dead and the gold of the syndicates would be worth less than its weight of pig lead.

Does Dr. McArthur and his crew now urge that this capital, nursed to life in the bosom of labor, shall, like the viper in the fable, destroy those who warmed and nourished it?

The fight is not between capital and labor. Without capital, labor would be like a Samson shorn of his locks, and honest labor is always willing that capital should have its just share of the profits. The fight is between labor and real capital on the one hand, and speculators, trust managers and international pawnbrokers on the other.

And, in the language of the Heralds of old, "May God Defend the Right!"

McKINLEYISM.—As a correct and clear definition of this term, we would suggest to future Dictionary-makers the following: The art of so taxing the poor that the rich may escape having to pay for the support of the government.

EDITOR CLARK HOWELL.

EDITOR CLARK HOWELL'S TRIBUTE TO BRYAN.

CHICAGO, Ill., July 11, 1896.

To THE EDITOR OF THE HERALD—

Whatever of good or bad there be in the demand for the free coinage of silver, the man and the movement met yesterday. A young man, too, but one year beyond the constitutional limit, and yet that man fired the Convention by the intensity of his eloquence as no man ever enthused an audience. Fresh from the bosom of the people, he sprang, a David, to give battle to the Goliath of the money power.

Fresh from the bosom of the people, he sprang, a David, to give battle to the Goliath of the money power.

A stripling from the West, girding his loins for the mightiest contest since the days of Andrew Jackson, has been called into the arena by the people to give battle to the stalking and silent champion of the monopoly which has cornered the gold of the world and which seeks to make its holdings the basis of the money supply of mankind.

The nomination of Bryan is an outburst of voluntary enthusiasm. He came heralded by no "managers," and accompanied by no retinue.

The nomination of Bryan is an outburst of voluntary enthusiasm. He came heralded by no " managers," and accompanied by no retinue. There was nothing premeditated or prearranged about it, and what has been done has been in response to the apparently all pervading sentiment of a Convention which in point of numbers as well as in the historic incident of the occasion, is the most remarkable which ever assembled in this country. Since Thursday the nomination of Bryan has been inevitable.

Before Thursday it was not considered as a remote possibility. His speech delivered in defence of the majority report of the Committee on Platform, did the work, and, with one accord, the silver men of the Convention think that the Democratic Moses has been found, and that the people have found the leader who is to save them from the relentless grasp of the hoarders of gold.

Not until now will the people be thoroughly convinced that a tidal wave is moving across the continent, but there will be abundant evidence to this effect between now and November. For nearly thirty years the Democratic party has burned incense on the altar of the party in New York, and during all that time Southern states have rolled up vast majorities for New York's nominee without quibbling or without question.

Even when they differed on economic problems the South and West have fallen in line with the East, and have submitted every question to the arbitration of the majority. If that decision was adverse, there was no sulking, no sitting by, with muffled mouths and threatening demeanor, but always the same enthusiastic, cordial and undivided support of the Democracy, which, for a quarter of a century, has gone to New York for its leader.

To-day the scene changes; New York's members take issue with the vast majority of the Convention; more than two-thirds of the body are of one way of thinking; New York sulks and sits, a silent and responseless listener to the call of the roll.

New Jersey and Connecticut do likewise; add parts of the delegation from Maine.   Delaware, Massachusetts and Vermont follow suit, but the convention proceeds with its business just as though the Eastern Democracy were again nominating a President, and all is well.   What the sullen and silent recalcitrants of to-day's Convention will do nobody knows—nobody cares.   Nominate another ticket and flock by themselves?   They can proceed without fear that they will be hurting anybody's feelings.

For every vote lost to the party by this step a hundred will be gained; for every State lost two are ready to take its place. For every vote lost to the party by this step a hundred will be gained, for every State lost two are ready to take its place.   Sooner or later it must be understood that the people of the whole country are in action and that they will not be led any longer as voluntary victims at the chariot wheels of the money power.

The country is now about to witness the most interesting campaign since the days of Clay and the elder Harrison. It will be a campaign of the hustings.   The campaign speaker will be in usual demand.   Every cross roads stump will reverberate with the echoes of campaign eloquence. New leaders will be found and new methods will prevail. It is money against patriotism, the flag against the three balls.   The people are in action, and the people will win.

CLARK HOWELL.

"The citizen who designates the money of the United States as dishonest should be disfranchised."—W. G. McLaughlin.

JUSTICE GAYNOR FOR BRYAN.

In a letter to General Almet F. Jenks, a leading law-yer of Brooklyn, he voices his sentiments on the political issues of the day.

BROOKLYN, July 14, 1896.

DEAR MR. JENKS:

It is a time for moral courage. Depend upon it, in this hour of weakness, hesitation and desertion, the great mind and heart of the unselfish, intelligent people is not falter-ing. Through mazes of sophistry and masses of im-material fact and fiction, their aggregate intelligence sees with sound vision ; and though some things may not be shaped in platform declaration as they would have them, nevertheless, they see and understand the main purpose, and are steadfast to it. Their ranks are not disordered by the shameless cry of "Anarchist" and "Socialist." Such free use is likely to provoke the inquiry whether the comparatively few who have in a generation or less amassed, and who are now amassing, vast inflated fortunes out of the public by the issuing of untold millions of fraudulent bonds and stocks upon public privileges and franchises, to pay in-terests and dividends upon which a proportionate tribute is levied upon nearly every community in the country— whether they are not the Anarchists, the endangerers of our institutions and social order, instead of those who think it wholesome and wise that such a state of things, and the unrest and demoralization caused by it, should not continue.

144

The parts of the platform against which this vulgar cry of " Anarchy " and " Socialism " is levelled, though not specified, are obviously those relating (1) to the money question, (2) to an income tax, and (3) to interference by the general government in local affairs. In respect of the first, the Republican platform expressly favors bi-metallism, but holds that it is impracticable in this country unless the other principal nations adopt it. The Demo-cratic platform holds that this nation is great enough to take the lead of the world in adopting it independently. Thus, both parties agree that it is better than gold mono-metallism. Is a bimetallist to be hooted at as an anarchist or lunatic?

Three years ago, in London, at the Mansion House, I heard Mr. Balfour make his great speech to a distin-guished audience in favor of bimetallism. I did not hear any one call him an Anarchist for so doing.

Those who say to us that the production of the two metals has since maintained about its former ratio, and that we can go back to the former condition and keep them at a parity as money, may, therefore—well, be at least decently listened to. Some are crying out for the sacredness of contract obligations, and for the national credit and honor, as though there was a suggestion to re-pudiate private or public obligations. All contracts pay-able in gold are inviolable under the Constitution. They cannot be changed by law.

All contracts payable in gold are inviolable under the Constitution. They cannot be changed by law. If our public bonds were, by their terms, payable in gold, they would have to be so paid. But they are not payable in gold.

The people of this country and of this state are for a tax upon incomes in excess of $4,000 or $5,000 by an overwhelming majority. It is the feeling even of the fair

and conservative rich that those who have the property of
a nation should pay its just proportionate share toward the
support of government which protects it. That is the sentiment of every nation in Europe as well as of this nation.
This cry from certain quarters of Anarchist and Socialist
against those who favor an income tax will not change
their minds. The fathers of many of them were abused
in the same senseless manner for speaking and voting
against human slavery.

No one can truthfully say that the allusion in the platform to the decision of the Supreme Court of the United States, declaring the recent income statute unconstitutional and void, is intemperate. No one can truthfully say that the allusion in the platform to the decision of the supreme court of the United States, declaring the recent income statute unconstitutional and void, is intemperate.
That decision of a divided court,
itself upset the previous solemn decisions of that court.
No court decision can permanently settle such a question
contrary to the mature judgment of the nation. Does any
one now say that the nation should have acquiesced in the
Dred Scott decision by the same court? It was thought
by those who hailed it with triumph to have settled forever
here the stability of human slavery, but instead it only
hastened the coming liberation of the slave. The people
would not have it.

There is left only the objection to local interference by
the general government. After the vehemence of those
called "old-line Democrats" against federal interference
of any kind, even to the supervising of federal elections,
which we have heard from boyhood up, this sudden cry of
Anarchy, especially by these "old-liners," against their
old doctrine, is strange enough.

These so-called leaders who are bolting would do well
not to be so conspicuous about it. What the people have

done for them, and how little some of them have done in return for the people, and what use they have made of political prominence and trust for their own personal aggrandizement, may come under a brighter light than they can bear. The combination of individuals, for instance, both in and out of the senate, who held up the Wilson tariff bill in the senate in the interest of the sugar, iron and coal trusts and combines, have not yet lost their identity in the public eye, whether they appeared openly, or masked behind dummies.

They will have a hard time to convince any one of their sincerity in now coming forward as the saviours of their party and of their country.   Yours very truly,

W. J. GAYNOR.

MEXICAN DOLLARS.

Amongst the many "bugaboos" flaunted in our faces by our gold standard friends, the threat that we will be deluged by Mexican dollars is a favorite with them. They do not tell us, however, that there are only $55,000,000 of them all told—rather a small amount with which to flood us. We must also bear in mind that there is a mintage fee of 2 per cent., and a stamp tax of 3 per cent. on all gold and silver carried to the Mexican mint.

Any comparison between the United States and Mexico which attempts to account for the difference between the two nations, on the ground that Mexico is on a silver basis, is entirely misleading.

PRESIDENT ANDREWS,

Head of Brown University, Declares Free Coinage Will Not Imperil Credit.

But National Bankruptcy, He Says, Will Follow a Continuance of the Present Gold Standard—No Influx of White Metal Likely—The Eminent Political Economist Disposes of a Number of Wall Street's Stock Arguments and Asks for Free Silver.

Rev. Henry W. Pinkham, pastor of the First Baptist Church, Denver, Col., and a friend of President Andrews, of Brown University, recently wrote to Dr. Andrews, asking these questions:

1. Do you favor the free coinage of silver at the ratio of 16 to 1 by the United States, without waiting for aid from other nations?

1. I do.

2. Could the United States, having adopted such free coinage, maintain the practical parity of the gold and the silver dollar?

2. I believe so.

3. Would not free coinage by the United States alone lead to a complete displacement of our gold? Why not?

3. I do not think so. People would not hoard or export gold in face of a movement certain to cheapen gold. It seems to me rather likely that the rehabilitation of silver by us would be the occasion of setting free vast amounts of gold now hoarded for military and other purposes.

148

4. Would not the effect of the recent increased production of gold as compared to silver be counter-balanced in the event of free coinage by the stimulus thus given to silver mining and by the influx of foreign silver?

4. This is partly answered under the last. Further, there would be no influx of foreign silver. Undoubtedly free coinage by us would increase the total amount of silver produced, but the new silver could not be mined at so low a marginal cost as at present prevails. The marginal cost would be on the contrary increased with the output, so that all tendency from this source to lower the gold price of silver would be negatived. The very prolific silver mines now are very few.

5. Would not the advantages of free coinage be more than negatived by the injury to our credit, thus causing a withdrawal of foreign capital?

5. Quite the reverse. After a possible first shock our credit would improve after free coinage. It is our present course which must speedily lower our credit. How long could a man or a firm continue to have credit who borrowed each year to pay a large portion of his running expenses? Yet on a gold basis this course is inevitable, and that is at this moment the reason why foreign lenders are shy of our securities. There must be a change if we would avoid bankruptcy. With free coinage every industry would look up, and even if we lost our gold our prosperity would invite in English capital, just as Japan's prosperity now causes it to rush there. Never since slavery days has the press in the parts of the country familiar to me, displayed such disregard for truth and such stubborn obtuseness to the most obvious considerations as it does at present on the silver question. This means that the money power seated in London, but with representatives in New York, Philadelphia and Chicago, is determined to continue the appreciation of gold, and determined therefore that the facts shall not be known. The bankers and the press are almost entirely under its influence. I think the money question at the present time the greatest question of civilization.

Yours, with kindest regards,

E. BENJAMIN ANDREWS.

The argument of Dr. Andrews is regarded as having the more importance because of his high standing as a financial writer. He has long been an advocate of bimetallism, but until recently urged international agreement. About two years ago he published a book called "An Honest Dollar" which was a plea for bimetallism, denying, however, the ability of the United States to bring this about without agreement with other countries.

Before becoming president of Brown University, Dr. Andrews was professor of political economy and finance at Cornell University.

BRYAN—SEWALL—PROSPERITY.

Protect the American people by permitting them, through the mints of their own Government, to coin their own money, and to issue it under the fiat of Uncle Sam instead of depending upon the fiat of any foreign government.

Why bond ourselves as slaves to the capitalists of the Old World?

Why not coin our own money out of the product of our own mines, and thus maintain the parity between gold and silver?

"Under the single gold standard prices in all gold standard countries are being driven down from day to day, from year to year. This drives down prices in the United States, and no protective tariff can prevent this fall of prices here and abroad." Hard times invariably follow in the wake of a falling market.

Secure the Restoration of the *Free Coinage of Silver and the Bimetallic Standard of the Currency,* and we can pay our bonds as easily in gold as we can now pay them in silver.

A Single Gold Standard furnishes no money except such as we can borrow from Europe, or such as we can procure there by selling our commodities to them at the price dictated by the owners of gold.

"THE CRIME OF 1873"—ITS HIS-TORY AND ITS EFFECTS.

"The demonetization of silver was the most gigantic crime of this or any other age ; it will cause more suffering to the people than if one-half of all the movable property, including railroads and shipping, were destroyed at a blow."—*John G. Carlisle's speech in the House of Representatives in 1878.*

The Act of Feb. 12, 1873, to which John G. Carlisle rightly applied the term "the crime of 1873," took away from silver the right to free coinage, which it had enjoyed from the foundation of our government up to that time, and it also took away from such silver coinage as might be issued by the government, the quality of legal tender, except in sums under five dollars. The direct effect of this was to reduce the material available for money by one-half. Previous to 1873, silver and gold were both available as money which required no redemption in anything else ; after that time, silver money was placed on a par with paper money, and was useful only in so far as it could be redeemed in gold. As the amount of silver and gold available for money had continued about equal in value for many years, this act of 1873 virtually lessened the money supply by one-half.

That this act was the result of a conspiracy planned years before and carried out with all the cunning and secrecy of experienced wire pullers, cannot be doubted by any calm and unprejudiced investigator who will trace its history.

The men who finally succeeded in destroying one-half the money of the commercial world began the work years ago, and it was a matter of indifference to them whether it was gold or silver that was demonetized, so that the quantity of money in existence should be lessened and all debts and obligations virtually doubled. Prior to 1849, things were in a condition quite satisfactory to these men, because the supply of the precious metals was little more than sufficient to meet the requirements of the arts and to compensate for the loss by abrasion, etc., and not at all equal to the increased demand made by a gradually expanding commerce. But when the gold discoveries of Siberia, Australia and California poured in their apparently unlimited supplies, the money kings took fright, and numerous treatises were written, advocating the demonetization of gold. Here, however, the conservatism of England stood the world in good stead. To demonetize gold in the rest of the world and leave England with her gold standard, would practically accomplish nothing. America, too, was intractable. To demonetize gold would be to greatly reduce the value of the products of the American mines just discovered in California, and American patriotism rebelled at the suggestion. Therefore, nothing was accomplished, and watching and waiting became the policy of the hour. The opportunity came in 1871, when Germany received the first instalment of the $1,000,000,000 indemnity from France in gold, or its equivalent. At the behest of the Rothschilds, whose agents in this country are the Belmonts, and who had advanced to Germany the sinews of war for the Franco-Prussian war, Germany adopted the gold standard and demonetized silver, and then the conspirators set to work to demonetize silver throughout the world.

The United States fell an easy prey. At that time

neither silver nor gold were in general circulation—paper being the medium of exchange. Sherman, Knox and Linderman set to work, and under the pretense of revising the mere system of the mint and the arrangement of the officers and their salaries, brought in a bill which effectually accomplished the work of the conspirators.

In the House, Mr. Hooper of Massachusetts repeatedly stated that the bill made no fundamental change in existing laws ; that it was merely a codification with a few alterations in regard to salaries, etc. This was clearly shown by the remarks of Senator Casserly of California, who said in a sort of interrogatory way : "This is a codified law," and John Sherman did not have the honesty to set him right. Everybody knows that a " codified " law is one which simply brings together and arranges in clear and logical form the laws already existing on the subject.

The bill as it finally passed was never read in the Senate. It is a long bill, covering fifteen pages of the book of statutes ; the reading was interrupted, and was never resumed. It was passed during the closing days of the session under a threat by Sherman that if the Senate attempted to discuss the bill, he would read to them certain correspondence of indefinite length, which would consume so much time that all other business would be paralyzed.

As Senator Daniel of Virginia said, "it went through Congress with the silent tread of a cat." The papers knew nothing about it. *Harper's Weekly*, which now shouts so loudly about " fraud," " repudiation," "anarchy," and "fifty-cent dollars," knew nothing about it. Nearly two years afterwards, on the 9th of January, 1875, Nast had a cartoon on the first page, in which the " Ark of State " is represented floating towards a distant mountain top which just appears above the deluge of waters, and is inscribed :

"On a Sound Specie Basis—Gold and Silver," while above a bright rainbow marked "Our Credit" spans the firmament. So that Nast, the illustrator, and Geo. William Curtis, the editor, one of the best informed men of his day, were both ignorant of the fact that Sherman and his gang had demonetized silver.

General Grant, who, as President, signed the bill, did not know that silver had been demonetized. Eight months after the passage of the bill, *viz.*, on the 3rd of October, 1873, he wrote to Mr. Cowdrey as follows :

" I wonder that silver is not coming into the market to supply the deficiency in the circulating medium. . . . Silver will become the standard of values, which will be hoarded in a small way. I estimate that this will consume $200,000,000 to $300,000,000 in time, of this species of our circulating medium. . . . I confess to a desire to see a limited hoarding of money. But I want to see a hoarding of something that is a standard of value the world over—silver is this."—*Forty-fourth Congress, 2nd Session. Report 703, page 89.*

Poor, deluded man! Honest, open and above board himself, he never suspected that a few sharp speculators had slipped through Congress and induced him to sign an act which for years would relegate silver to the class of pig metals!

In the face of all this, what is the value of the long tabular statement of Prof. Laughlin, giving the number of times some bill on the subject was brought up and discussed ? The fact is that the bill which the professor describes is not the one that was passed and which became law. That bill which was a substitute bill, and passed as such, was never read at all.

After the United States had demonetized silver, and Germany had thrown a large amount of her old silver coinage on the market as bullion, France, Belgium, Italy, Switzerland and Greece became alarmed and closed their mints to silver. This, of course, took away all coinage demand for the metal, and the price gradually sank until, in 1893, the Indian mints were forced to close. After that the descent was rapid and the price of silver fell from $1.29 per ounce, in 1873, to 63 cents per ounce in 1894.

The effects of this " crime " are known to all. It has made millionaires on the one hand and tramps and paupers on the other. The prophetic words of John G. Carlisle, quoted at the head of this article, did not overdraw the evils and miseries of which it has been the cause, and although Mr. Carlisle has deserted the cause of the people and humanity, and has allied himself with trusts, monopolies and money-changers, his words, so far as they rest on facts, appeal to our knowledge and experience as well as to our reason.

JAMES G. BLAINE SPEAKS.

James G. Blaine, speaking on the floor of the House, Feb. 7, 1878, said :

" I believe gold and silver coin to be the money of the Constitution ; indeed, the money of the American people anterior to the Constitution. which the great organic law recognized as quite independent of its own existence. No power was conferred on Congress to declare that either metal should not be money. Congress has, therefore, in my judgment, no power to demonetize silver, any more than to demonetize gold."

The reader will find the history of this conspiracy given more fully on another page of this book.

WHO WAS THE CRIMINAL?

In a recent interview with Murat Halsted, Senator John Sherman, referring to "the crime of 1873," said :

"The crime of 1873, with which I am charged, was unlike the crime of 1806, which Jefferson committed, in this, that he ordered the coinage of silver dollars stopped, and in 1873 the order for coinage of legal tender silver when the mint regulations were revised, was not given."

It will be seen that Mr. Sherman here plainly acknowledges that there was a crime, and, like other bad little boys, he tries "to put it on to the other fellow."

How was it ?

At the time that President Jefferson ordered the director of the mint to cease the coinage of dollars and to coin only half dollars, quarters and dimes, the country was poor and greatly in need of currency. The dollar was a favorite coin with many of the nations with which we traded, and as fast as the mint turned them out they were exported, so that *the people* got no benefit from them. Jefferson, being a true Democrat, took the side of the people, and ordered that no piece above the half dollar should be coined. This had a tendency to keep silver in the country, and this was the reason distinctly and expressly given in the letter to the director of the mint, written under Jefferson's direction by Secretary Madison, and dated May 1st, 1806.

But these half dollars, quarters and dimes were full and unlimited legal tender for all debts public and private and, to quote the words of the statute in force at that time and for a quarter of a century afterwards, "it was lawful for any person or persons to bring to the said mint, gold and silver bullion in order to their being coined ; and that the bullion so brought shall be there assayed and coined as speedily as may be after the receipt thereof, and that free of expense to the person or persons by whom the same shall have been brought."

In these free coinage and full legal tender silver pieces there was coined $76,734,964.50, and that during a time when the population was small and the country comparatively poor. So that it cannot in any correct sense be said that silver was demonetized by order of Jefferson. Mr. Sherman cannot get rid of the charge in that way, by shoving it on to Jefferson.

Such papers as the New York *Evening Post* and the New York *World* have repeated over and over again the statement that there were only about 8,000,000 silver dollars coined prior to 1873, and that since that time 430,790,041 have been coined. This is technically true, but practically false. Prior to 1853 there was coined over $84,000,000 of full legal tender and free coinage silver.

The silver coined after 1873 was not under free coinage, and while it was unlimited legal tender (except the subsidiary coins) it was mere credit or token money and served no purpose which might not have been equally served by the same weight of fine bronze worth say thirty cents per pound. And for this state of things John Sherman is almost wholly responsible. The secrecy and mendacity which characterized the passage of the law of Feb. 12, 1873, which demonetized silver, probably cannot be parallelled in the history of legislation. The bill which *actually* passed was never read in Congress ; it went through both houses with "the silent and stealthy tread of a cat," and the very President (Grant) who signed it and made it a law, did not understand its effects. The latter statement has been recently denied by his son, but Grant's own letter is on record, and is given on another page of this book.

During the civil war the gold owners managed to make money out of both sides and to accumulate fortunes at the expense of both the North and the South. At the North they managed to get back three dollars for every dollar that they lent the government, and this was done largely by "rigging the market," as it is called. Sometimes, however, they did not succeed as they expected, as the following amusing anecdote told by Ben. Butler, in his book, shows:

"On Thursday evening, it having been generally circulated in the city that General Butler had shut himself up in his headquarters and dared not show himself lest he should be assassinated, I sent an officer of my staff to take a stage box for us at the opera, having got a new uniform so that I could go in full feather. We appeared there, and were received with some applause, which I acknowledged. I sat out the entertainment. Between the acts Captain DeKay, of my staff, who was a society man in New York, left the box to visit one wherein he saw his aunt, and found therein Mr. August Belmont. Mr. Belmont made a statement publicly in his hearing that he would bet a thousand dollars that the election would go for McClellan, and another thousand that gold would go up to 300 by the morning of election. This being reported to me, I told Captain DeKay to say to Mr. Belmont that those bets would be taken; but Mr. Belmont declined."

Gold did not go up to 300, but Mr. Belmont's vote was challenged on account of his bets, and he did not vote. Belmont acted as the agent of the Rothschilds and "worked both sides for all they were worth."

THE TRADE DOLLAR.

In his speech at Columbus, O., on the 15th day of August, 1896, Senator John Sherman, referring to the proposed free coinage of silver, used the following language:

" It is harsh to express this opinion of a measure favored by many good people, but I cannot regard it in any other light but as both a fraud and a robbery, and all the worse if committed by a great, rich, and free people. A citizen who should commit such an offense would be punished by the courts or denounced as dishonest, but a nation like ours, is beyond the power of any tribunal but conscience and God."

Such an earnest and emphatic condemnation of anything bearing even the semblance of repudiation must be gratifying to every right-minded citizen. But when Mr. Sherman charges fraud and repudiation upon those who would undo the evil results of the great conspiracy of 1873, of which he was an active aider and abettor, he totally misapplies the terms. None of the prominent advocates of the free coinage of silver propose either fraud or repudiation in any form whatever. What they demand is simple justice and honesty—no more, no less.

But there did occur a case of repudiation pure and simple which it may be well for the people of the United States to call to mind as it may throw some light on the character of the men now most prominent in hurling charges of repudiation against those who are striving to undo the great wrong committed by Sherman and his party. Let us here briefly give the facts:

In his report to the Secretary of the Treasury, dated Nov. 19, 1872, at which time the famous bill known as "the crime of 1873" was pending in Congress, Dr. Linderman, then Director of the mint, recommended the manufacture of a disk or ingot of silver weighing 420 grains 900 thousandths fine. This disk or coin was intended to compete in China and the East with the Mexican dollar, and thus make a market for American silver, and it was expressly recommended that it be not made legal tender. But John Sherman, who had charge of the coinage bill in the Senate, called it the "trade dollar," named it as one of the coins of the United States, and made it legal tender to the extent of five dollars. Under such conditions about 15,000,000 of these coins were issued, and it will require very little knowledge or reflection on the part of the reader to convince him that every one was a distinct obligation on the part of the United States; in other words, being issued as legal tender, they had the same force as if the United States had issued 15,000,000 one dollar checks or bills.

Things went along very well until silver began to fall in price, and then Mr. Sherman recommended that the legal tender quality be taken away from these "trade dollars." In other words that they be repudiated, and this was done by joint resolution dated July 22, 1876. It would of course, have been easy, and also perhaps just, to have taken away the legal tender quality from all such coins as might be issued *after* that date, and 20,000,000 of them were afterwards made for the trade with the East. But to take away the legal tender quality from coins already issued, and which the people had consequently been forced to accept, was precisely the same as if the

United States had issued an equal number of checks or one dollar bills and then repudiated them.   John Sherman suggested and recommended this very course.   See his speech delivered in the Senate, April 11, 1876.   This speech is also reproduced in his collective speeches, published by the Appletons in 1889, and the passage to which we refer will be found at page 523 of that book.

These trade dollars, as many of our readers may remember, obtained a very considerable circulation amongst mechanics and small business men.   When they fell in value and were no longer legal tender they were sold to the bullion brokers at a discount of from 10 to 30 cents each.   This loss fell upon the common people, and, to use John Sherman's words, "We cannot regard it in any other light but as both a fraud and a robbery."

But this was not the whole of it.   In 1887 a law was passed authorizing the redemption of these trade dollars at their full face value, without any regard to whether they had been issued as legal tender or not !   This law was engineered through Congress by a syndicate that had bought up all the trade dollars they could find and had also bought up a number of U. S. Senators by admitting them to the pool " on the ground floor."

"The most common and meanest argument against a measure is that it will help somebody."—John Sherman's Speech in the Senate, June 8th, 1876.

HOW IS THE WORKINGMAN TO BE BENEFITED BY THE FREE COINAGE OF SILVER?

" For my part, I am willing to state here that if Mr. Bryan could show me that by any means known to heaven or known on earth, any means revealed to the comprehension of man, that wages could be increased, I will be ready to support him here and now."—*Bourke Cockran in his Speech at Madison Square Garden.*

It is an economic principle as firmly established and as clearly demonstrated as any of the great truths of physical science that no important class of the community can be injured without inflicting injury upon the entire nation. And the converse is equally true ; you cannot, by just means, increase the prosperity of any important class without increasing the prosperity of all. Mr. Cockran, like the partisan and demagogue that he is, sets this great principle at defiance, and attempts to array the Southern cotton planter and the Western farmer against the mechanics, the railroad men, and those engaged in professional pursuits. Talking here to the mechanics and manufacturers of the East, he urges them to vote for McKinley, so that they may have high wages and cheap living, forgetting that if the farmer and the cotton planter cannot get fair prices for *their* products, they cannot buy the products of the mechanic and the manufacturer, and consequently the latter will labor in vain.

In order that there may be good wages there must be a market for the things produced by the wage-earners, but how can there be a market when those who ought to be purchasers are unable to buy? The fatal sophistry of the McKinleyites lay in their argument that if the farmers would only vote for high protection, they would have a paying market for their products. Pay a little more for your coats and plows and railroad iron, and we will find a home market for your wheat and beef and cotton! They got the protection, but the profits went into the pockets of Hanna, Carnegie, Rockefeller and their syndicates.

On the other hand, the promise to the mechanics was that under high protection the farmers would buy such quantities of goods that the mills and factories would all be kept running full time. What was the result? In the home city of the Republican candidate for vice-president, a city of 80,000 inhabitants, more than half the working population are idle to-day.

And it must be borne in mind that the wealthy gold advocates—the Whitneys, the Martins, the Goulds, the Van Alens, the Morgans, the Belmonts, and Bourke Cockran make no market for American products. These and their kind go to Europe every year or two, spend there millions of the wealth produced by American labor, and then return laden with the products of European tailor-shops, bric-a-brac, ladies' dresses, etc., *which they import duty free as personal effects.* One family brought over one hundred and twenty trunks filled with such goods, and they were admitted duty free because they were decided to be not out of keeping with the station in life of the persons who brought them in! A poor man bringing them in would have had to pay the lawful duty.

And thus doth protection protect!!

Mr. Cockran would build up wages and pull down the farmers, but the motto of every true democrat is

" Live and let live."

Good prices to the farmers, fair wages to the mechanics and other wage-earners, and work for all.

Will free coinage aid in bringing about these conditions? We think it will, and for the following reasons :

Since the demonetization of silver there is not enough *actual* money to transact the business of our rapidly increasing manufactures and commerce. The only reply ever made to this proposition by the advocates of gold is that of one of their ablest writers, Mr Horace White, editor of the *Evening Post*, and better known, perhaps, as "Coin's Financial Fool." His only reply is the counterquestion: "How do you know?"

A very little explanation will make the truth of our statement clear to all except men of the class of Bourke Cockran and Horace White.

All commerce is simply barter, and money is merely the tool by which the barter is effected. The merchant does not really sell his goods for money, but for other goods and articles of value ; the farmer does not raise crops merely for the sake of getting money, but for clothing, stock, tools, land, or the discharge of mortgages and debts. Even the mechanic does not work for money, but for food, clothing, shelter, etc., and money is merely the tool which enables the merchant, the farmer and the mechanic to exchange their goods, products and services for what they really need. If a mechanic or a farmer buys too many tools, he wastes his wealth; if he has not enough tools, he works at a disadvantage and loss. The carpenter who has only a cross-cut saw, and tries to do all his work with it, loses more time and effort than would buy several sets of saws ; the farmer who is short of plows, and is obliged to let his men and horses stand idle because they have not tools with which to work, will soon be bankrupt. It is the same with money. If the supply of money should be short, the business of the country is carried on at a disadvantage, and this is the case at present.

But say the gold advocates: "Look at the banks; in all the great money centers the banks have more money than they know what to do with." Very true, but it is not actual money. It is that credit money which comes from the deposit of checks and the discount of notes. When a merchant gets a note discounted at his bank, he does not draw the money; he gets a credit on the books of the bank against which he draws checks, but the bank has no more money than before, although perhaps $10,000 has been added to its deposits.

This will be seen more clearly if we examine the Reports of the Comptroller of the Currency.

Taking the report for 1892, the amount of the deposits in the national banks alone was $2,296,076,185. In other words, the merchants and other customers of the banks had this amount of money to their credit, and were entitled to draw checks against it. But according to the Report of the Director of the Mint for the same year, there was only $1,649,547,000 actual money in the country. This included gold, silver, nickels, copper and paper of all kinds. Of this real or actual money a large amount was in the pockets of the people, the tills and safes of merchants, etc., not to speak of the large quantity in the vaults of savings banks, state banks, trust companies and large corporations.

So that while the *apparent* amount of money on deposit may be very large, the actual amount may be so small as to be within the danger line. This is the case at the present time. The banks have an immense amount of *credit* money on deposit, but the proportion of *real* money is so small that the banks actually talk of issuing clearing house certificates to protect themselves in case of a panic.

Moreover, the banks have so much credit money on hand that it would be imprudent for them to increase it, and consequently they are compelled to refuse all loans and discounts. It is currently reported that one of the foremost houses in New York was refused discount on three months' notes at nine per cent., and in the home city of the millionaire Republican vice-presidential candidate, an old established manufacturing concern, whose wealth and credit were unimpeachable, was refused discount at eight per cent. Is it any wonder that our stores, shops and mills have to close and that merchants, clerks, mechanics and mill-hands are thrown out of work ?

The only remedy for this is to increase the supply of actual money, and this can be done only through the restoration of the free coinage of silver. If the credit money now on deposit in the banks can be backed up with a little more actual money, the merchants will buy from the manufacturers, the manufacturers will set their mills going, the wage-earners will find employment and good pay, and the farmers will find in the wage-earners, people who are ready and able to buy their products. Can anything be clearer than that free coinage is what is wanted to start the wheels of industry and so benefit the wage-earners ?

MR. BRYAN'S TIVOLI ADDRESS.

" Mr. Chairman, Ladies and Gentlemen : The presence of a number of persons who are prepared to discuss at length the issues of this campaign, together with the fact that I have considerable work ahead of me, will make it unnecessary for me to occupy a great amount of your time. But I appreciate this opportunity of presenting to you, even briefly, some points which I deem worthy of your consideration.

" We are entering upon a campaign which is a remarkable one in many respects. Heretofore, at least in the last twenty-five or thirty years, each party has gone into the campaign practically solid, presenting a united front against the opposing party. But in this campaign there has been practically a bolt from every convention which has been held. What does this mean ? It means that convictions are deeper this year than they have been heretofore.

"It means that people are not so willing now as they have been to allow the platform of a party to control their **Men are thinking this** action. Men are thinking this **year with more of earn-** year with more of earnestness and **estness and intensity than** intensity than they have in recent **they have in recent years.** years, and the results of this thinking will be manifested when the time comes to register the will of this great nation, and between that time and this hour we expect to present to those who must act upon the questions the issues of this campaign.

" When our party at Chicago wrote the platform, which

167

it did, we knew that it would offend some people. No
party can take a plain, strong, emphatic position upon
any question without offending somebody. We declared
in that platform what we believed was right. We declared
there the policies which we believed were best for the
American people, and when we did it we knew that it
would alienate some.

"Let me read one of the planks of that platform :

"'We are opposed to the issuing of interest bearing
bonds of the United States in time of peace, and condemn the trafficking with the banking syndicate which, in
exchange for bonds, and at an enormous profit to themselves, supply the Federal Treasury with gold to maintain
the policy of gold monometallism.' That is one of the
planks. That was not put in there **That was not put in**
to attract love of those who have **there to attract love of**
grown rich out of the Govern- **those who have grown**
ment's extremities. (Applause.) **rich out of the Govern-**
We did not expect those who **ment's extremities.**
have a passageway from the Federal Treasury to their
offices to join with us in closing up the passageway.
(Applause.) We did not expect those who are making a
profit out of a gold standard and out of the embarrassment
which it brings to the Treasury to join with us in putting
an end to the gold standard. Why, if we had expected it,
we would have expected it in the face of all the history of
the past.

"Do you remember the Good Book tells us that some
1800 years ago a man named Demetrius complained of
the preaching of the Gospel? Why? 'Why,' he said,
'It destroys the business in which we are engaged. We
are making images for the worship of Diana, and these
people may say that they be not gods that are made with
hands.' But Demetrius was much like men who have

lived since his day. When he had made up his mind that the preaching of the Gospel interfered with his business he didn't go out and say to the world, 'Our business is being injured and we are mad.' What did he say? He said, 'Great is Diana of the Ephesians.'

He didn't go out and say to the world, "Our business is being injured and we are mad." What did he say? He said, "Great is Diana of the Ephesians."

"We have some to-day who are very much like Demetrius. They know that the restoration of bimetallism destroys the business in which they have been engaged.

They don't say that the Democratic party is wrong because it interferes with our business. What do they say? They say: "Great is sound money; great is an honest dollar."

"But when they make public speeches they don't say that the Democratic party is wrong because it interferes with our business. What do they say? They say 'Great is sound money; great is an honest dollar.' (Applause and laughter.)

"I say this platform was not written to attract their votes. It was written because we want to destroy the business in which they are engaged. But, my friends, if those who have made a profit out of the government's financial policy array themselves against the Democratic party, may or may we not expect those who believe that we are right to come to our rescue and fill up the ranks that are being thus depleted? If we must part company with those who believe in a government of syndicates, by syndicates and for syndicates, may we not appeal with confidence to those who believe that a 'government of the people, by the people and for the people should not perish from the earth?' (Applause.)

"If these men who pride themselves upon their prominence in the business world, and who glory in the title of business men, are going to make a business out of politics,

I beg you to consider whether the great toiling masses of this nation have not a right to make a business out of politics once and protect their homes and their families.

are going to use their ballots to increase their incomes, I beg you to consider whether the great toiling masses of this nation have not a right to make a business out of politics once and protect their homes and their families. (Applause.)

"I have not been in the State of New York long. I have not met many of your people. And yet in the short time that I have been here I have met enough Republicans who have told me that they were going to vote our ticket to make up for every prominent Democrat that has deserted us. (Applause.) And we welcome the coming guests as we speed those who are parting. (Applause.)

"Now, my friends, this is a practical question. It is a question which you must consider for yourselves. The gentleman who has preceded me has very properly told you that you are competent to settle this question for yourselves. The founders of our government never conceived that a time would come when there would be only a few people in this country who would be competent to

If they had they would have written in the Constitution that on most questions everybody could vote, but on the money question, only the financiers could vote.

settle a great public question. If they had they would have written in the Constitution that on most questions everybody could vote, but on the money question only the financiers could vote. (Applause and laughter.) It is hollow mockery to grant to the people a right in your Constitution and then deny them the privilege of exercising the right.

"I assert that the people of the United States, those

who produce wealth as well as those who exchange it, have sufficient patriotism and sufficient intelligence to sit in judgment upon every question which has arisen, or which will arise, no matter how long our government may endure. (Applause.) The great political questions are economic questions, and great economic questions are in their final analysis great moral questions, and it requires

It requires no extended experience in the handling of money to enable a man to tell right from wrong. no extended experience in the handling of money to enable a man to tell right from wrong.

"And, more than this, this money question will not be settled until the great common people act upon it. No question is settled until the masses settle it. Abraham Lincoln said that the Lord must have loved the common people, because he made so many of them. (Applause.) He was right about it. There is another evidence that the Lord made the common people, and made a great many of them.

The common people are the only people who have ever supported a reform that had for its object the benefit of the human race. It is because the common people are the only people who have ever supported a reform that had for its object the benefit of the human race. (Applause and cheers.) I do not mean to say that there

have not been exceptions to the rule. I do not mean to say that you have not found among the masses at all times those who are ready to betray those who toiled with them if they could see some chance of personal elevation. Nor do I mean to say that those who have got beyond the ranks of the common people are entirely unmindful of the claims of brotherhood upon them. But I say, as a general rule, that the common people here and everywhere have been the support, and the only great support, of every measure of reform. (Applause.) Now you have a right to take this question, examine it, and form your own opinion, and the ballot is given to you in order that you may express your own opinion when you come to vote, and not be required to accept somebody else's opinion.

The ballot is given to you in order that you may express your own opinion when you come to vote, and not be required to accept somebody else's opinion.

"And I am going to call your attention to just a few things this afternoon for you to consider when you are trying to make up your minds what you are going to do.

"Now our opponents are all divided as to the policy which should to be pursued. You take the gold standard Democrats, some of them say they ought to come out openly and indorse the Republican candidate, so as to be sure and elect him ; others say 'No, that would be dangerous, because unless we have a canditate of our own there will be a great many Democrats who will be foolish enough to vote the Democratic ticket.'

"And there they are divided. They all want the same object. They all want to elect the Republican candidate, because they believe that Democracy is better exemplified through Republicanism (laughter and applause) than through Democracy.

They all want to elect the Republican candidate, because they believe that Democracy is better exemplified through Republicanism than through Democracy.

"But I say they are divided as to the means of getting at it, and some say that they can elect the Republican candidate better by having a candidate of their own to fool Democrats with than they could by openly supporting the Republican ticket.

"Not only are they divided there, but they are divided all the way through when they come to argument. Why, some of them will start out to show that the gold standard is a good thing, and after one of their speakers has got

well on showing how great a thing the gold standard is,
then another speaker comes along and says it is a mistake
to say the gold standard is good; the gold standard is not
good : what we want is bimetallism, but we can't have it
until somebody helps us.   Now those two arguments are
not consistent.   If the gold standard is not a good thing,
why should they want bimetallism ?   And yet if they ever
have two men making speeches
the same night, the chances are
16 to 1 that one of them will
praise the gold standard as a good
thing, while the other will tell you
how anxious they are to get rid
of it.   Well, then, they come to
the details of the argument.   One
man says the reason why he does not want free coinage is
that he does not think that the Government should pass
a law that will enable a silver miner to take 50 cents
worth of silver bullion and convert it into a hundred cents
and make the difference.

"And he will get red in the face, become indignant at
the idea that the Government should attempt to help some
individual in this way.   Of course he may have been in
favor of a system of taxation that would yield 200 or 300
per cent., but that doesn't count.   It is a terrible thing to
allow the silver miner to make that profit.   Then the next
man who comes up will say that as a matter of fact the
stamp of the Government adds nothing to the value of
the metal, and that the free coinage of silver simply
means that you convert 50 cents' worth of bullion into a
50-cent dollar, and nobody makes any profit out of it.
(Laughter.)

"I say that the chances are, that if you have two men
make speeches on the same platform in favor of our not

taking any action until some foreign nation helps us, you
will find that one of them will in all probability make one
argument, and the other will make the other argument,
and very often the same man makes both arguments.
(Laughter and applause.) Now you can see the absurdity
of it.   If the silver miner, under the law of free coinage,
finds that his silver bullion is raised so that that which is
now worth 50 cents will be worth 100 cents, then there are
no 50-cent dollars, and if the other man is correct, and
the law adds nothing to the value of the metal, and you
simply convert 50 cents' worth of silver into a 50-cent dollar, then the mine-owner has not made a cent. (Applause.)
If there are two men to speak against our position, one
of them will probably say that there has been no fall in
prices, and he will denounce the people who complain
that gold has risen in price, and after he has proved that
to the satisfaction of every man who does not think, then
his colleagues will come on and tell you that, not only
have prices fallen, but that it is the greatest blessing in
the world to have prices fall.   (Laughter and applause.)
Those two are not consistent, but it follows all the way
through.   Why is it ?   It is because our opponents have

Our opponents have no
theory, no principle, no
policy upon which they
are prepared to stand
and fight.
no theory, no principle, no policy upon which they are prepared
to stand and fight.   They do
not dare to say that the gold
standard is a good thing, because
no party in the history of this country has ever declared
in favor of a gold standard ; and they do not dare to say
that it is a bad thing, and then tell seventy millions of
liberty-loving people that they have got to suffer until
some foreign nation comes and brings them relief. (Applause, and a voice, " That is right.")

" I want you to remember that in the discussion of this

money question there are certain fundamental principles; and when you understand those principles you understand the money question.

"I was out in a portion of the country where they irrigate on a large scale, and I found enormous plants, and investigating them this thought occurred to me : What principle is it that underlies the subject of irrigation ? There is a principle that you must understand before you can do anything in the way of irrigation. What is the great underlying principle? It is that water runs down hill. (Laughter.) Until you learn that, you cannot do anything toward irrigating a farm; but when you understand that water runs down hill, then all you have to do is to dig a ditch with a slant to it, and you can carry water wherever you want to. (Laughter.)

When you understand that water runs down hill then all you have to do is to dig a ditch with a slant to it, and you can carry water wherever you want to.

"Now, so it is with the money question. You have got to find out the fundamental principles which underlie the subject, and when you understand those principles you understand the money question. What is the principle that underlies it all? It is that the law of supply and demand applies to money as it does to everything else.

"You know that if the world's crop next year of a certain article is very much greater than the crop this year, that article will fall in price ; if the crop is much smaller than this year, the article will rise in price. You know that the law of supply and demand reaches and controls money, as well as other forms of property. It reaches and controls all sorts of property.

"Increase the amount of money more rapidly than the demand for money increases, and you lower the value of a dollar; decrease the quantity of money, while the demand for it increases, and you increase the value of a dollar. When you understand that, you understand the essence of the money question. When you understand that, you understand what its effect is on you; and then you can tell where your interest lies. When you understand that principle, then you understand why the great crusade in favor of the gold standard finds its home among the holders of fixed investments, who, by such legislation, raise the value of the property which they hold.

Increase the amount of money more rapidly than the demand for money increases, and you lower the value of a dollar; decrease the quantity of money while the demand for it increases and you increase the value of a dollar.

The great crusade in favor of the gold standard finds its home among the holders of fixed investments, who, by such legislation, raise the value of the property which they hold.

"I am not giving you my authority for it; I can quote you authority which our opponents dare not question. I have called attention, and I shall continue to call attention to a remark made by Mr. Blaine in Congress on this subject. He said that the destruction of silver as money, and the establishing of gold as the sole unit of value must have a ruinous effect upon all forms of property, except those investments which yield a fixed return in money; that these would be enormously enhanced in value and would gain a disproportionate

The destruction of silver as money and the establishing of gold as the sole unit of value must have a ruinous effect upon all forms of property, except those investments which yield a fixed return in money, that these would be enormously enhanced.

and unfair advantage over every other species of property. (Great applause.)

"There is a statement that no man who has respect for his reputation will dare to dispute, that the establishing of gold as the sole unit of value throughout the world and the destruction of silver as standard money means that you shall destroy the value of all property except money and investments that call for a fixed amount of money. It means that you will give to those investments and to this one form of property, money, an advantage over every other form of property.

"When you understand the effect of the policy and then understand that the desire for it is manifested most among those who hold the fixed investments or trade in money, I think you will come to the conclusion that I have come to—that the fact that the gold standard is a good thing for them is the principal reason why they are in favor of a gold standard. (Applause.)

When you make up your minds that the gold standard is a bad thing, then the only question that you have to consider is, how can you get rid of it? "When you make up your minds that the gold standard is a bad thing, then the only question that you have to consider is, how can you get rid of it? Our opponents may raise objections to the plans which we propose, but I want to suggest that you are interested not so much in knowing the objections to our plans as in knowing what plans they have to relieve the condition. (Great applause.) Why don't they propose something? Is it because they don't know what ought to be done? If so, they are poor people to lead you out of bondage. (Laughter and applause.) Is it because they know and will not tell? If so, they have not the candor that should be possessed by those who would redeem a people from their suffering and distress. (Applause.) They say that our dollar will be a 53-cent dollar. They refuse to apply to the silver that is produced in the world the law of supply and demand. We say, increase the demand for silver by legislation, and that new demand, acting with the demand now in existence, will operate upon the price of silver. We say that that new demand will be sufficient to consume all the silver presented at the mint, and being sufficient, will raise the value of silver bullion to $1.29 per ounce throughout the world. (Applause.)

" We have a reason for our belief : They simply say, ' It won't do it, it won't do it,' and then sit back and propose absolutely nothing.

" I have known some of our opponents to use this sort of argument : Why, they say, if the free coinage of silver makes a silver dollar equal to a gold dollar, it will be just as hard to get a silver dollar as it is to get a gold dollar. Do you know what they overlook ? They overlook the fact that when we bring silver into competition with gold and increase the supply of standard money, that, while a silver dollar will be worth as much as a gold dollar, it will be easier to obtain, with the products of toil, a silver dollar, or a gold dollar, than it is to-day. (Applause.) Our complaint is, that the same hostile legislation which has destroyed the demand for silver and driven down the price of silver when measured by gold, has also increased the demand for gold, and driven up the price of gold when measured by other forms of property, and that the opening of our mints to the free and unlimited coinage of silver will operate to bring more money into circulation, and thus lessen the strain that has existed for gold, and that by increasing the demand for silver, we bring silver up until silver and gold meet at the ratio now fixed by law, and a silver dollar and a gold dollar will be of the same value here and all over the world. (Applause.) But I have spoken beyond the time that I expected to. (Several voices : "Keep on; go on !"   Another] voice: "We will stay here till to-morrow morning.")

"I simply want to say this: If there is any person here who is afraid that under the policy proposed by the Chicago platform we are going to have a flood of money and that you will be drowned in it, we cannot appeal to him for support. (Laughter.)   But if there is anybody here whose experience is such that he is willing to risk the disastrous consequences of that flood upon him, we ask you to consider whether we are not entitled to your vote." (Applause.)

A voice :   "Are you a Democrat ? "

"I think that the principles which I advocate are Democratic."

A voice :   "Right you are!"

Another voice: "You are a Democrat."

"I call myself that, but you may call me any name you please; you cannot swerve me from what I believe to be good for the people. (Continued applause and cheering.)

"My friends, I want you to study this money question for yourselves, and I want you to understand that if bimetallism is to be restored, the United States must take the lead. (Applause.)

"We have waited for more than twenty years to have the benefits of bimetallism brought to us by those whose interests are opposed to ours. I assert that the American people not only have the right, but have the ability to legislate for themselves on every question, no matter what other nations may think about it. (Great applause.)

We have waited for more than twenty years to have the benefits of bi-metallism brought to us by those whose interests are opposed to ours.

"The man who says that bimetallism is desirable and yet that the United States is impotent to bring its advantages to our people, has made an admission that I shall not make. (Applause.)

"We appeal to you to remember that the United States is the only nation that stands ready to protect its own people from every danger, foreign and domestic.

Foreign nations may protect their people, as they should, but our nation is the only nation that can protect the American people.

"Foreign nations may protect their people, as they should, but our nation is the only nation that can protect the American people. (Applause. A voice: "That's right.")

"If we need relief from the gold standard we must secure it ourselves, and if we must secure this relief for ourselves we can only secure it through a party which believes in the immediate restoration of the free and unlimited coinage of gold and silver at the present legal ratio of 16 to 1, without waiting for the aid or consent of any other nation." (A voice : "That's right." Great applause and cheers.)

WILL FREE COINAGE BRING FIFTY=CENT DOLLARS AND REPUDIATION?

The methods of reasoning adopted by the gold advocates are frequently very remarkable, and, to the ordinary mind, incomprehensible. Thus they tell us that it is not fair to allow a miner to take fifty cents' worth of silver to the mint and have it coined into a dollar worth 100 cents, and then in the next breath they tell us that these 100 cent dollars, when put in circulation, are worth only fifty cents! If all this were true, it would be a sort of legerdemain which would throw the feats of Houdin and all the great conjurers entirely into the shade. These people are afraid that somebody will gain some advantage from free coinage, and, as John Sherman says, one of the meanest and commonest of all arguments against a measure is that it will help somebody. We sincerely hope and believe that free coinage will help the miner, the farmer, and the mechanic. If we did not believe so, we would work against it with might and main.

Let us then try to find out what will be the effect of free coinage on the value of the silver dollar as compared with the dollar of gold?

This is a purely economical question which can be answered in advance of actual trial only, by a consideration of such sound, economical principles and well-ascertained facts as are applicable to the case, and it is on this line that we propose to try to give an answer.

The director of the mint tells us in his last report, that the amount of silver in use as money in the world is $4,070,500,000, and some of the gold men tell us, that to keep the silver dollar at par with gold, all this silver must be raised from 68 cents per ounce to $1.29 per ounce, a task which they say is utterly beyond the ability of any one, or even two countries, in the world, not excepting the United States.

Much of this silver, however, is already held at a price which is *above* $1.29 per ounce. Thus Great Britain has $115,000,000 which she holds at $1.44 per ounce, and no man could put a grain of this silver on the market at $1.29 per ounce, without losing the difference between $1.29 and $1.44. France has $58,000,000, which she holds at $1.43 per ounce, and $430,000,000 which she holds at $1.33 per ounce. Other nations have large amounts held at varying prices, all above $1.29, so that a syndicate that would attempt to buy up the $4,000,000,-000 of silver in the world with the hope of selling it to the United States at $1.29 per ounce, would find themselves subjected to a loss which, even to the Rothschilds, would be no trifle.

On examining the statistics of the question, we find that the silver of the world is held as given in the following table. What is called "limited legal tender," may be defined as the "change-money" of the world—the shillings and sixpences of England, the dimes and quarters of the United States, and the small coins of France. These are absolutely necessary in the transaction of business, and the amount required will increase rapidly, rather than diminish.

Amount of Silver held by the Gold-using Countries, and the rate at which it is held:

Limited legal tender, $631,200,000 @ about $1.40 per oz.

France	430,000,000 "	1.33	"
Belgium	48,000,000 "	1.33	"
Italy	21,400,000 "	1.33	"
Switzerland	10,000,000 "	1.33	"
Greece	500,000 "	1.33	"
Germany	105,000,000 "	1.48	"
Spain	136,000,000 "	1.33	"
Austro-Hungary	80,000,000 "	1.49	"
Netherlands	53,000,000 "	1.30	"
Turkey	30,000,000 "	1.30	"
Cuba	1,500,000 "	1.33	"
Hayti	2,100,000 "	1.33	"
Bulgaria	3,400,000 "	1.33	"
United States	548,400,000 "	1.29	"

$2,090,500,000

Here, then, we have $2,090,000,000 in silver held considerably above our par, by gold and gold and silver using countries which could be brought to the U. S. mint only at a heavy loss. This leaves $1,980,000,000 for use in the silver-using countries where it is held at a valuation of 53 cents on the dollar. Of this

Mexico has	$55,000,000
Central American States	12,000,000
South American States	30,000,000
Japan	68,000,000
India	950,000,000
China	750,000,000
Straits Settlements	115,000,000

$1,980,000,000

Now this silver is all in use as *money* in these countries; to withdraw even a small percentage of it would cause such a contraction as would raise the market value of the rest to such a degree as would quickly bring it up to $1.29. Even Mexico, poor as she is, could not part with 10 per cent. of her currency without severe suffering. All that we would have to do would be to absorb 10 per cent. of the silver of the silver-using nations, and silver would go up.

And it is a curious fact that the amount of silver which would be thus brought to our mints is just about the amount of the national bank notes now in circulation. Withdraw the national bank notes, and replace them with $200,000,000 of silver under free coinage and full legal tender, and the thing is done.

But here, by way of parenthesis, the writer of this article cannot but think that the people of the United States in general, and the Chicago convention in particular, make a great mistake when they confound banks and bankers with money-lenders and money-brokers. The Rothschilds, the Belmonts, the Morgans, and men of their kind are not BANKERS in the true sense of the word. They are merely pawnbrokers on a large scale. Banks and bankers are as necessary to a community as grocers and dry-goods dealers; a well-conducted bank is one of the most efficient agents that can be devised for advancing the prosperity of a community, but men like the Morgans, Belmonts, etc., are mere parasites on the body politic, and when they are called "bankers" the term "banker" is degraded, and legitimate banking business is brought into disrepute. It is to the interest of real banks and bankers that business should prosper, for it is in good times that they make most money. But money-lenders and pawnbrokers always thrive best when the people are in distress.

The reply which is invariably made to this, is that
we have tried it and failed; that we have bought not
only $200,000,000, but $548,400,000, and that, in the
face of this purchase, silver sank to 63 cents per
ounce.

The fatal error which vitiates this reply consists in the
implied assertion that the silver thus purchased is money.
With the exception, perhaps, of the subsidiary coinage,
we have not a single dollar of silver money now in use in
the United States.   Every dollar is based on gold, and
the silver might just as well be bronze, leather or paper.
So long as the credit of the United States is pledged to
keep silver at a parity with gold, the silver dollars in circulation are merely so many promises stamped on silver
instead of paper, and the more of these dollars we issue
the greater is the burden on gold, and the higher is the
value of gold raised.

But to raise the value of gold is precisely the same thing
as to lower the value of silver and all other commodities;
and, therefore, in the long run, the effect of the Sherman
law was precisely the opposite of what some of its advocates expected.

After a slight rise, due to the *expectation* of the increased
value which was believed to be coming, silver fell to the
lowest price ever recorded.

We must bear in mind that in matters of money some
of the economic laws seem to be reversed, because money
is, in a certain sense, the converse of commodities. Thus
while everybody knows that good jack-knives will, at the
same price, drive out poor ones, it is equally true, though
not so generally well known, that poor money, at the
same valuation, will always drive out good money; and
this is but one illustration out of many that might be cited.
The Sherman law, therefore, tended to ultimately lower

the price of silver, not to raise it, as free coinage would
have done.

Free coinage of both gold and silver kept the two metals
nearly at a parity for two hundred years, as the reader
may see by consulting the last Report of the Director of
the Mint.   For the convenience of our readers, we give
the ratio year by year since the establishment of our
mint.   It will be seen from this that during that time the
ratio never fell below 15 to 1, which was our ratio during
the first forty years of our coinage, and that prior to 1873
it never rose above 16 to 1, except during the year 1812,
when it rose to 16.11.

To those who are familiar with the history of the cur-
rencies of Europe this table furnishes an exceedingly in-
structive subject for study.   Bearing in mind the fact that
our ratio was changed twice, being 15 to 1 up to 1834, then
16 to 1 up to 1837, and then 15.98837 up to the time of
demonetization ; bearing also in mind that the French
ratio was 15.5 to 1, and that several nations had different
ratios, it is really surprising that the average ratio kept so
even.   During the early part of the century the commerce
of the world increased much more rapidly than the supply
of money, and the discoveries in California, Australia, and
Siberia came just in time to rescue humanity from the
grasp of the money-lenders of that day.   But the need for
money made either silver or gold acceptable, and, as will
be seen from the table, the immense supply of gold caused
but a very trifling change in the ratio.   In 1871, Germany
demonetized silver, but as France and the Latin Union, as
well as some other countries, still kept their mints open,
the ratio still kept near 15.5.   But when these mints were
closed, in 1873 and 1874, the fall was rapid.

It must be borne in mind that while the mints were
closed to silver they were still open to gold.   This acted

Commercial Ratio of Silver to Gold each year since the passage of our first Coinage Law in 1792:

YEAR	RATIO	YEAR	RATIO	YEAR	RATIO
1791	15.05	1826	15.76	1861	15.50
1792	15.17	1827	15.74	1862	15.35
1793	15.00	1828	15.78	1863	15.37
1794	15.37	1829	15.78	1864	15.37
1795	15.55	1830	15.82	1865	15.44
1796	15.65	1831	15.72	1866	15.43
1797	15.41	1832	15.73	1867	15.57
1798	15.59	1833	15.93	1868	15.59
1799	15.74	1834	15.73	1869	15.60
1800	15.68	1835	15.80	1870	15.57
1801	15.46	1836	15.72	1871	15.57
1802	15.26	1837	15.83	1872	15.63
1803	15.41	1838	15.85	1873	15.92
1804	15.41	1839	15.62	1874	16.17
1805	15.79	1840	15.62	1875	16.59
1806	15.52	1841	15.70	1876	17.88
1807	15.43	1842	15.87	1877	17.22
1808	16.08	1843	15.93	1878	17.94
1809	15.96	1844	15.85	1879	18.40
1810	15.77	1845	15.92	1880	18.05
1811	15.53	1846	15.90	1881	18.16
1812	16.11	1847	15.80	1882	18.19
1813	16.25	1848	15.85	1883	18.64
1814	15.04	1849	15.78	1884	18.57
1815	15.26	1850	15.70	1885	19.41
1816	15.28	1851	15.46	1886	20.78
1817	15.11	1852	15.59	1887	21.13
1818	15.35	1853	15.33	1888	21.99
1819	15.33	1854	15.33	1889	22.10
1820	15.62	1855	15.38	1890	19.76
1821	15.95	1856	15.38	1891	20.92
1822	15.80	1857	15.27	1892	23.72
1823	15.84	1858	15.38	1893	26.49
1824	15.82	1859	15.19	1894	32.56
1825	15.70	1860	15.29		

in two ways; it not only depressed silver, but it raised
gold.   It was like taking a vote from one candidate and
giving it to another; the effect is to make a difference,
not of one vote only, but of two.

We have not space here to discuss all the effects of these
successive occurrences, but we feel assured that no man
can study the table of ratios which we give without coming to the conclusion that the opening of our mints to silver will bring the two metals very nearly, if not quite, up
to the ratio of 16 to 1.

"Until six years ago I thought anybody was a crank who
talked about money, but when I got to study the money question, I found that it overshadowed all other questions, and that
it was deeper and greater and higher than all other questions
which we had to deal with."—W. J. Bryan.

"I believe that the gold standard is made up of more misery
for the human race than wars and pestilences and famines,
more misery than human mind can conceive or human tongue
can tell, and I shall cry out against it as long as God gives
me the voice to speak."—W. J. Bryan.

"I assert that property rights, as well as the rights of persons,
are safe in the hands of the common people. Abraham Lincoln,
in his message sent to Congress in December, 1861, said: 'No
men living are more worthy to be trusted than those who toil up
from poverty; none less inclined to take or touch aught which
they have not honestly earned. "—William J. Bryan, at Madison
Square Garden.

THE FREE COINAGE OF SILVER NO MENACE TO PROSPERITY.

THE campaign of 1896 will be distinguished from all that have preceded it by the intensity of the educational influences at work. It will be essentially what has been called a campaign of education, and the practical decision of the people will undoubtedly depend upon the opinions which they will form in regard to a great economic question. Both candidates are men of pure lives and honorable conduct. Even such bitter opposition papers as the *Evening Post*, the *World*, and the *Sun* of New York, acknowledge that Mr. Bryan is above reproach. A correspondent of the *Evening Post*, writing from the vicinity of Mr. Bryan's home, says of him, that "he is a clean, wholesome fellow," and attributes his political successes in his own State to "his oratory, in which he has few equals, and I doubt if any superiors," and also to the fact that "the people of his district believed that he was thoroughly sincere and honest."

Those who will compare the speeches of Mr. Bryan and Mr. Cockran, delivered in Madison Square Garden, must see that Mr. Bryan is no demagogue. His speech was calm, dignified, logical and based on sound economic principles; Mr. Cockran's speech was a pyrotechnic display of vituperation, misstatements, bad logic and error. He attempted to array section against section, while, as every one knows, the prosperity of this country must stand or fall as a whole. You cannot have successful mechanics and impoverished farmers; if you injure the cotton-planter and the western agriculturist you destroy the best market available to the eastern wage-earner. On the subject of political economy his ignorance was simply pitiful. He denied the fundamental principles of monetary science, as when he told us that the purchasing power of money does not depend upon its quantity—a principle laid down by Aristotle, Copernicus, Locke, Hume, and all the older writers, and enforced by John Stuart Mill, who says : "The value of money, other things being equal, varies inversely as its quantity. * * * That an increase of the quantity of money raises prices, and a diminution lowers them, is the most elementary proposition in the theory of currency, and without it we should have no key to any of the others."—*Principles of Political Economy, Book III., Chap. VIII.*

No more influential campaign document could be issued by the Democratic party than the speeches of Bryan and Cockran arranged together in the "deadly parallel."

There cannot be any doubt that the question upon which this campaign will turn will be the proposed return to the free coinage of silver, and a consequent addition to the money supply of the world.   That such an increase always brings prosperity is a truth as old as the science of money itself.   It has never been put into more distinct and forcible language than in the words of Hume, the famous historian, who said: "We find that in every kingdom into which money begins to flow in greater abundance than formerly, everything takes a new face; labor and industry gain life, the merchant becomes more enterprising, the manufacturer more diligent and skilful, and even the farmer follows his plow with greater alacrity and attention."

Now, Hume was not writing as a political partisan, or as the advocate of any "crank" theories.   The above was a deliberate conviction reached after careful historical study (in which department Hume occupied a foremost place, as his famous " History of England " shows), and presented in a calm, philosophical " Essay on Money," which stands as an accepted authority to this day.   And the soundness of Hume's conclusions are fully moved by the financial history of the United States.   Whenever we have had an increase in the money of the country we have had prosperity; when, by reason of panics and bank failures, the currency was contracted, hard times came on.   It was so in the years prior to 1837, and to 1857, and the contraction in these years came from the inability of the banks to maintain their issues at par, because there was too much credit money in proportion to actual money. This difficulty can never arise in the case of free coinage, because metal to which the mints are open is always at par.

The times prior to 1873 were times of expansion, caused by the use of a paper currency which was not convertible into silver or gold, but they were times of prosperity.   On Feb. 12, 1873, the act demonetizing silver was passed, and by midsummer of that year we had one of the most severe panics in the history of the nation.   This panic was not directly due to the demonetization act, but the coincidence was a curious one.   Hard times set in, and continued for some years, the country gradually recuperating as is usual in such cases. In 1878 the Bland-Allison law was passed, whereby $2,000,000 were coined every month, and we had good times for some years. Then the Sherman law was passed, by which 54,000,000 ounces of silver a year was pur- chased, and the purchase money added to the circulation. This did no harm until the howls of the gold men caused European investors to take fright and return our securities. This took away the gold reserve, upon which not only the legal tender pa- per, but the silver itself (to the extent of nearly $600,000,000) rested, and as the silver in the treasury was of no more use than so much pig lead, the treasury was powerless to protect it- self, and the panic became daily more acute. To this cause must be added the action of certain large moneyed corporations, who not only called in some of their loans, but advanced the rates of interest to borrowers. At last, in 1893, the Sherman law was re- pealed, all purchases of silver on government account were sus- pended, and the panic began to abate.

The whole monetary legislation of this period was the practical embodiment of absurdity. Congress passed a free coinage law, but this was vetoed by the president. Then the government pur- chased silver, issuing paper for it, a most unprecedented course, and one which was of advantage neither to the silver owners nor to the people, because both in law and practice the silver was maintained at the mint value by redemption in gold, and conse- quently the entire weight of the money function still rested on gold. Practically the effect of this was to diminish the supply of silver by so much as was bought, and to increase the demand for gold by just the same amount. The silver gave no more re- lief than so much paper would have done, and the burden placed on gold was increased, and its value was raised, and of course this meant that the value of silver was lowered.

Through all this battle the two most bitter enemies of silver were John Sherman and Grover Cleveland The outcome is that both these men are multi-millionaires, while the average pay of the wage-earners of the United States is forty cents per day, if we accept the figures given by Mr. Bourke Cockran in his Madi- son Square Garden speech.

Against the irresistible logic of these facts the gold advocates oppose nothing but vituperation, and the senseless epithets of " repudiators," " socialists," and " anarchists." Thus, amid the

innumerable misstatements and absurdities which compose the
recent speech of Bourke Cockran, we find the following : "He
[Bryan] is a candidate who declared that this is the beginning of
a revolutionary movement, but no sooner found himself face to
face with the American feeling than he realized that this soil is
not propitious to revolution !"

This was a strange statement to make in the very home of revolution ! Revolution is the potentiality of progress. This nation
was born in a revolution, and has lived in a state of revolution
ever since. There has not been a decade of its existence that has
not seen a revolution which has relegated some old creed, or some
worn-out system to oblivion; and this has gone on until a country
which, less than one hundred years ago was, in large part, the
home of savage beasts, and still more savage men, is now the
most civilized and progressive nation on the face of the globe.
From the Atlantic to the Pacific it is pierced with railroads, net-
ted with telegraph wires, and dotted with schools and churches,
and where, but a few years ago, the bison and the panther found
a lair, we now find cities which rival the cities of old in magnifi-
cence, and citizens who far excel in intelligence and refinement.

But, as a matter of fact, Mr. Bryan and his supporters suggest
no revolution. What they do suggest, is a return to a system under
which we had our greatest prosperity, and which will again bring
not only prosperity, but justice.

The campaign of 1896 will be the most memorable in all the
long history of this country. As a campaign of thorough education in sound political economy, it has never had an equal. Men's
hearts and minds are stirred to-day as they have never before been
stirred in the history of the country. The battle of the Middle
Ages is about to be fought over again, and this time to a finish;
but the contest will not be between mail-clad warriors and stubborn yeoman attempting to wrest from their oppressors the
glorious privileges of a magna charta, but between the subtle
forces of plutocracy on the one hand, and true civilization on
the other. We use these terms with a full apprehension of their
meaning, for every thoughtful man knows that wealth and true
civilization are not only far from synonymous, but that they are
frequently antagonistic. Luxury is not true refinement, and real
intellectual progress is never fostered by vast wealth.

The dark ages followed a period of the most luxurious wealth ever recorded in the history of humanity, and to-day the drift of society in the United States is toward a repetition of the closing scenes of the Roman Empire.

We find the age of luxury creeping on apace, and the children of American cabinet officers, instead of following the example of the Fathers of the Republic, trying to outdo Lucullus, a Roman whose very name has become a synonym for luxurious extravagance. What were the feasts of Lucullus compared with that $50,000 dinner given in Paris by a young American to a few of his boon companions, while thousands of his fellow-countrymen, although living in a land of seeming plenty, scarcely knew where to get to-morrow's frugal meal?

It has been well said that history repeats itself, and in nothing is this more fully verified than in the Sherman crime of 1873. Seventeen hundred years ago the plutocrats and money-lenders of that day adopted the same tactics that the Rothschilds, Belmonts, Morgans, Whitneys and Benedicts have pursued. By an imperial edict, issued in the year 221 of our era, silver was declared to be no longer money, and gold was made the only legal tender for debts. The creditor classes soon had all the wealth of the country in their grasp. The people were reduced to actual slavery, and were sold with the lands and the mines, as so many attached cattle, and the dark ages settled down over humanity.

The people of the United States have at last awakened to the true condition of things. They realize that, in the words of the author of "Common Sense Currency":

" While a mistake in regard to the tariff, or an error in the matter of taxation, would be to the body politic what a severe wound, or the amputation of a limb, would be to the human system, an unsound currency is to a nation what blood-poisoning is to a man: it permeates every fibre, paralyzes every function, and, unless cured, brings death and destruction."

They now propose to study the subject carefully, and vote intelligently. This will not be an election carried by boy-like shouts of irrelevant and meaningless cries, or even of party shibboleths. The people are pretty sure to consider the matter carefully and earnestly, and in the language of our candidate : " Each citizen must study the question for himself, and as he does so he must remember that he is responsible for the vote he casts."

www.ingramcontent.com/pod-product-compliance
Lightning Source LLC
Chambersburg PA
CBHW030839270326
41928CB00007B/1135